SHOUT, SISTER, SHOUT!

Ten Girl Singers Who Shaped a Century

ROXANE ORGILL

MARGARET K. McELDERRY BOOKS
New York London Toronto Sydney Singapore

Margaret K. McElderry Books
An imprint of Simon & Schuster Children's Publishing Division
1230 Avenue of the Americas
New York, New York 10020

Book design and shoe illustrations by Anne Scatto / PIXEL PRESS

The text of this book was set in Electra.

Printed in the United States of America

10 9 8 7 6 5 4 3 2

Library of Congress Cataloging-in-Publication Data
Orgill, Roxane.
Shout, sister, shout! Ten girl singers who shaped a century / Roxane Orgill.
p. cm.
Includes biographical references (p.) and discography (p.).
Contents: The 1900s : Sophie Tucker, the last of the red hot mamas — The 1910s : Ma Rainey, mother of the blues — The 1920s : Bessie Smith, empress of the blues — The 1930s : Ethel Merman, la Merm — The 1940s : Judy Garland, the girl next door — The 1950s : Anita O'Day, jazz gypsy — The 60s : Joan Baez, sibyl with guitar — The 1970s : Bette Midler, the last of the real tacky ladies — The 1980s : Madonna, material girl — The 1990s : Lucinda Williams, ramblin' woman.
ISBN 0-689-81991-9
1. Women singers — United States — Biography — Juvenile literature. 2. Popular music — United States — History and criticism — Juvenile literature. [1. Singers. 2. Women — Biography.] I. Title.
ML400 .O74 2001
782.42164'092'273 — dc21
[B]
99-054374

For Conrad

CONTENTS

ACKNOWLEDGMENTS

M Y FIRST THANKS go to George Nicholson, my literary agent and a man of ideas, with whom I developed the idea of a collective biography of "girl singers."

I wish to thank the New York Public Library for the Performing Arts, an invaluable resource. The librarians in both the circulating and research collections were most helpful to me.

Barbara Seuling and the members of her writers' workshop provided guidance and criticism at all the right times.

Thanks to Michael Gillespie, who shared with a stranger his treasured photographs and programs of Bette Midler, and to Miller Williams, father of Lucinda Williams, who rooted through the family photo collection for me.

Lastly I thank Charles Hamm, a professor of music history at the University of Illinois in 1975, who played a recording of Bobby Short singing "Just One of Those Things" and turned my classical-music head around.

INTRODUCTION

If I should take a notion
To jump into the ocean
'Tain't nobody's bizness if I do.

BESSIE SMITH sang those lines in 1923, but they would be appropriate for any of the "girl singers" in this book, at any time during the twentieth century. This book tells the stories of ten women who went about their own business, regardless of what other people said or did. These women took charge of their lives and their singing careers, with the possible exception of Judy Garland, who spent most of her difficult life under the thumb of others. But she, too, triumphed in the end: She is probably the best known of all of the singers here.

This book concentrates on just ten performers out of easily a hundred candidates who qualified as "great singers" in the United States from the years 1900 through 1999. How to choose just ten?

First of all, they had to be terrific singers whose voices I wanted to listen to over and over. That doesn't necessarily mean they had great voices. The jazz singer Anita O'Day did not have much of a vocal instrument, certainly as compared to her better-known contemporary, Sarah Vaughan. But what Anita did with her little voice was more interesting to me than what Sarah did with her magnificent one.

Each woman had to have an interesting story to tell. How did she become a singer? Did she take charge right away, or did others manage for her? What stood in her way and how did she get around it, or push it aside? In each of the ten stories I tell here, a woman struggles to make the most of her musical gift.

The singers represent ten different genres of popular music and entertainment. Sophie Tucker was a "red-hot mama" in vaudeville, Bette Midler a rock singer who found her niche in cabaret. Joan Baez sang folk songs, and Judy Garland starred in movie musicals. Every singer in this book made a significant contribution to her genre as well as to the culture in general.

The book is organized by decade, with one singer per decade. Each singer appears in the decade in which she did her best or most prolific work. Pairing a singer and a decade was a challenge for the 1990s, which were still rolling as I wrote. Suddenly I was no longer dealing with history but with the present. How was I to know which of the top performers would still be considered exceptional ten, twenty, thirty years from now? The solution: Chapter 10 focuses on "three faces" of country music, with Lucinda Williams, a singer-songwriter on the fringe of mainstream country, as the central figure, and two hugely popular crooners, Wynonna Judd and LeAnn Rimes, in sidebars.

Following these criteria meant leaving out many wonderful performers, including some of my—and, no doubt, the reader's—favorites. Rosemary Clooney, whose recordings I'd take to that imagined desert island where you're allowed only one or two treasured possessions, is not in the book. She was best known in the 1950s but did her most acclaimed work in the 1980s and 1990s, and she did not, I feel, represent the events and national mood of those decades. Aretha Franklin is also not here, because I felt her story was too thin, perhaps because she is a private person and has yet to reveal much of her past. A popular singing trio from the 1920s and 1930s, the Boswell Sisters, also didn't make the book, but Connee Boswell and her siblings, Vet and Martha, did record a song in 1931 whose title,

"Shout, Sister, Shout," captured exactly the sentiment I had about the work of my chosen singers and thus inspired the title of this book. The list goes on: Barbra Streisand, Doris Day, Mahalia Jackson, Peggy Lee, Whitney Houston, Ella Fitzgerald, Janis Joplin, Billie Holiday, Patsy Cline, and Linda Ronstadt—to name just a handful of other great voices. I apologize for their absence.

How do I know a great singer from a not-so-great singer? I come to this book from more than twenty years as a music critic for newspapers and magazines, including the *Wall Street Journal*, the *New York Times*, the *Milwaukee Journal*, the *Bergen County* (New Jersey) *Record*, and *Billboard*, to name a few publications. I began studying music as a child by playing the violin, and continued my studies in college and graduate school, where I concentrated on music history and theory. Along the way I found I loved writing about music. It's a challenge to attempt the impossible, that is, to put music into words. If I do the job well, a person might go out and listen to something new, or hear an old favorite in a new way.

My training was in classical music, and popular music is a relatively recent, thrilling discovery for me. Pop music in all its diversity is one of this country's richest and most lasting contributions to the world. It is my hope that by book's end, the reader has some sense of the music's progress across the century and the pleasures it offers. As Madonna sang, "Cel-e-bra-ate." Read the stories, then go find their recordings. Listen to these ladies sing. They have so much to tell us.

—R. O.
Hoboken, New Jersey
August 2000

Starting out in vaudeville in the early 1900s, Sophie Tucker signed the mat bordering this photograph, "Noisy Sophie Tucker."

SOPHIE TUCKER

The Last of the Red-hot Mamas

SOPHIE TUCKER peered from behind the curtain. It was two o'clock, show time, at Tony Pastor's Theatre in New York City, where big-time agents came to look for new acts of vaudeville. The seats were empty! "What's the matter?" she asked a stagehand.

"It's always like this," he said. "They don't start coming in till after two-fifteen."

At 2:28 the pianist played the introduction to her first song, and Sophie went out and started to sing. She was overwhelmed by the sudden tramp of feet coming down the aisles, the rattle of wooden seats as they were folded open, and the talking and laughter of arriving patrons. She stopped singing. The piano fell silent. Her robust voice shot across the footlights. "What for you-all so late gettin' in hyar? Hyar I am all dressed up and with some most special songs you-all ain't never heard yet. Don't you-all know you're keeping the show waitin'?"

She got a big laugh. What's more, she got the audience's attention. After five songs, the audience clamored for more. Sophie wondered later, "Where did I get the nerve to holler out like that to a New York audience?"

If there was one thing Sophie Tucker was never short on, it was nerve. Nerve propelled her from her family's restaurant in Connecticut, where she waited on tables and sang the occasional song, to New York City and show business. Eventually, nerve got her into big-time vaudeville, and not just as one of fifteen or sixteen acts in a show but as a "headliner"—one of a handful of performers who saw their names shining in electric lights on theater marquees across the country.

Her timing could not have been better. In 1908, when Sophie was twenty-one and shouting down the audience at Pastor's Theatre, vaudeville was fast approaching its peak as the most popular form of entertainment in America. Nearly every town had at least one vaudeville theater where traveling troupes performed a variety show at very low prices. People went once, even twice a week. And why not? For a quarter or fifty cents, you might see a strong man who could tear a telephone book in half; a boxing kangaroo; a pair of comedians; a one-act play; eight dancing girls; a troupe of talented mules; or a female singer in a glamorous gown. Some twenty thousand vaudevillians were traveling the railroads on their way from one theater to the next. Among them was bawdy songstress Eva Tanguay (whose theme song was "I Don't Care"); escape artist Harry Houdini; the brother-and-sister dance act of Fred and Adele Astaire; Will Rogers, the cowboy who roped a horse onstage; ventriloquist Edgar Bergen and his smart-aleck dummy, Charlie; and "The Twelve Speed Maniacs," who assembled a Ford automobile in two minutes flat. And there was Sophie Tucker, whose big, belting voice "put the trombone in its place and made the electric lights flicker"—or so it was said.

Sophie was a large, buxom woman. She wore her golden hair piled on her head and, once she was earning big money, favored extravagant clothes: long, flowing dresses, dainty shoes with ribbon bows, lots of diamond jewelry, and a feather headdress that shot up eighteen

Pastor's Theatre on Fourteenth Street, New York City, where Sophie Tucker appeared in blackface in 1908. The sign says seats cost twenty and thirty cents. The marquee on the sidewalk reads: "Tony Pastor's High Class Vaudeville."
(BILLY ROSE THEATRE COLLECTION, THE NEW YORK PUBLIC LIBRARY FOR THE PERFORMING ARTS, ASTOR, LENOX AND TILDEN FOUNDATIONS)

inches into the air. She always looked elegant, even queenly. And yet in her manner she was anything but aloof. She was open and kindhearted, a pal to everyone. She could tell bawdy jokes without offending people—important in a clean, family entertainment like vaudeville.

Sophie was born on January 13, 1887, somewhere in Poland. Her mother was emigrating from Russia to America with her baby son when she went into labor in a wagon. The wagon driver left them by the side of the road. Fortunately, people in a nearby house took in mother and son, and delivered Sophie.

Three months later, the family joined Sophie's father in America. To evade Russian authorities, he had changed his last name from Kalish to Abuza. He settled in Hartford, Connecticut, where he opened Abuza's Home Restaurant.

Everybody in the Abuza family worked. Sophie got up at three o'clock in the morning to wipe the frost off the salami and bologna and to slice bread for sandwiches. She wrapped her feet and stuffed the front of her dress with newspapers to keep out the cold. Then she did housework, ran errands, and peeled vegetables for soup *before* going to school. If she fell asleep every morning in geography, she was wide awake during music class, and was often called on to lead the singing. After school she waited on tables.

One day when she was about eleven, Sophie sang "Break the News to Mother," a popular song about a dying soldier, for the customers. The song brought tears to many eyes and extra tips to Sophie. Her father got excited and told his wife, "You see, someday, with that great big voice of hers, she'll make big money for us."

At the city park concerts, Sophie began to accompany—on the piano with one finger—her younger sister Anna, who sang. Then something marvelous happened. "I was going on thirteen, and already I weighed about one hundred forty-five pounds," Sophie recalled. "I was gawky and self-conscious. Gradually, at the concerts, I began to hear calls for 'the fat girl.' Then I would jump up from the piano stool, forgetting all about my size, and work to get all the laughs I could get." She picked up jokes at Poli's Vaudeville Theater in her hometown. She learned songs from the show people who came into the restaurant, who scribbled the lyrics, not

Sophie Tucker in her early twenties, posing for a publicity photo: "In show business clothes matter," she said.

the music, on scraps of paper for her. "I couldn't have read the notes if I had had them," Sophie said. "And I had no need of them. I was born with a quick and true ear."

When she was about seventeen, a young man named Louis Tuck asked Sophie to a dance—her first. Two months later, she married him. They had a son, Bert. Tuck worked as a driver for a horse-drawn beer truck, but brought home little money because he gambled. He, Sophie, and their son moved in with her parents, and Sophie went back to working in the restaurant. When she told Tuck to take care of his family and get a better job or leave, he left. The marriage had lasted two years. Sophie, meanwhile, saved one hundred dollars from singing and, in the fall of 1906, she begged two weeks' vacation and left baby Bert with her parents. She had no intention of returning. She wrote her parents from New York City: "I have decided to go into show business. I have decided that I can do big things and have definitely made up my mind that you will never stand behind a stove and cook any more, and every comfort that I can bring you both I am going to do, and I know I can do it, if you will let me alone."

Sophie found a room for five dollars a week, including breakfast, and a restaurant that would let her sing for her supper. She changed her name to Sophie Tucker, because "Mrs. Tuck didn't sound right for a singer," she said. Sophie was completely dedicated, even to a job that paid only in food, not cash. "Every morning I turned out of bed and marched myself up to the music publishers' and got the pianists to go over new songs with me."

"Got something new, boys?" was her standard greeting. Already she had formed the philosophy that was to serve her for fifty years. "From those days to this my motto has been: 'Get something new. Keep fresh. Don't get stale, singing the same songs.' I made it my job to learn all the new popular numbers as they came out and to have these with me."

Sophie had her eye on German Village, a classy restaurant on West Fortieth Street, that employed fifteen to twenty singers. When the manager told her she was too young, she bought a new outfit "on time" (paying one dollar a week until the full payment was reached), put her hair up, and got the job. She sang as many as one hundred songs a night for fifteen dollars a week plus tips. True to her word, she sent a weekly money order to her family.

Sophie then landed a spot on Chris Brown's amateur night, a place far uptown on 125th Street, where newcomers could be seen by agents booking the vaudeville circuit, and her career took a sharp turn. As she was about to go onstage, Mr. Brown said, "This one's so big and ugly the crowd out front will razz her. Better get some cork and black her up. She'll kill 'em." An assistant quickly rubbed burnt cork on Sophie's face, ears, and neck. He painted on a grotesque mouth with lipstick, tied a red bandanna over her hair, and thrust a pair of black cotton gloves on her hands.

Just like that, Sophie became a blackface comedian. "Blacking up" to look like a Negro was a popular vaudeville tradition, practiced by whites and blacks alike. Blackface actors performed caricatures of blacks, typically a bumbling, ignorant type known as a "coon." Singers who blackened their faces and sang Southern songs

What's New?

Records

The twelve-inch 78 revolutions-per-minute (rpm) record was introduced in 1902. It held up to four minutes of music. The same year, Italian singer Enrico Caruso, then a young tenor at the La Scala opera house in Milan, made a handful of recordings that made him millions of dollars and brought him international fame. Other opera singers, impressed by the new and improved recording methods, followed suit. On the popular side, Billy Murray quickly made a name for himself by recording songs from Broadway musicals that became standards: "You're a Grand Old Flag," "Give My Regards to Broadway," and "By the Light of the Silvery Moon."

Silent Movies

The first "story picture," a silent movie that told a story, was shown in theaters in 1903. Called *The Great Train Robbery* and directed by Edwin S. Porter, the movie lasted ten minutes and employed such new technical tricks as the close-up.

What Was Vaudeville?

Vaudeville, whose heyday ran from about 1900 to 1930, was an inexpensive form of entertainment for the average person. Its chief appeal was its fabulous variety. The bill changed every Monday: new performers, new music, new acts, and marvels.

What could you see? If you were poor in 1908, you could go to The People's Vaudeville in New York City and, for five cents—the price of a loaf of bread—you saw three silent films, two vaudeville acts, and a singer accompanied by slides projected on a screen. If you had cash to spare in 1913 you could visit the brand-new Palace Theatre, on Broadway at Forty-seventh Street, where the best seats cost two dollars. There you would see nine acts: La Napierkowska, a dancer, in *The Dance of the Bee;* a condensed version of an operetta called *The Eternal Waltz;* a cartoonist; a violinist from the Spanish Court; a one-act comedy; the Four Vannis, a high-wire act; a one-man comedy sketch; McIntyre and Harty, singing comedians; and eight London Palace Girls, a dance troupe.

Vaudeville was supposed to be wholesome entertainment for the whole family, and theater managers were responsible for eliminating anything from acts that people might find offensive, like the word "devil," for which the word "dickens" was substituted. When Sophie Tucker made her debut at the Palace in July 1914, one story relates that she failed to heed the bulletin posted by the manager. It read in part: REMEMBER THIS THEATER CATERS TO LADIES AND GENTLEMEN AND CHILDREN. VULGARITY WILL NOT BE TOLERATED. One of her numbers—"Who Paid the Rent for Mrs. Rip Van Winkle (When Rip Van Winkle was Away)?"—was deemed unsuitable for "ladies and gentlemen and children," and she was canceled after one performance. She was invited back to the Palace in 1925, when she introduced the more suitable and, ultimately, fabulously popular "My Yiddishe Mama."

were called "coon shouters." Today it's hard to find the humor in such openly racist gestures, but at the time, blackface had appeal to both races—for different reasons. Anyone, black or white, could enjoy feeling superior to a fool, but black audiences got an extra kick out of seeing white folks' "imitations" of black people. When the actor was black, the humor became more complex: Blacks laughed at a black blackface actor making fun of the white blackface actor who imitated black folks.

"All right, you're on," said the stagehand. Sophie felt sick with fright. The pianist thumped out the opening chords, jolting her out of her fear. She strode onstage and sang three songs, which the audience liked so much, they refused to let her go until she had sung three more.

On the way home that night Sophie recognized a booking agent on the subway train. She went up to him, her face still sooty. "You heard me sing?" she asked. "Did you like me? Do you think you could book me?"

Yes, he did. Sophie spent the next year on the small-time circuit of second-rate theaters in New England for thirty-five dollars a week. Despite the low pay, she was thrilled to be in her first vaudeville job and described herself as "a big, husky girl, carrying her own suitcase, attending to her own railroad tickets, boarding places, looking out for herself, as capable and independent as a man." It couldn't have been easy to manage as beautifully as Sophie did. The vaudeville life was rough and it was lonely. Performers typically stayed a week in one theater, and took a train on Sunday night to the next town on their schedule. They ate poorly. "Home" was a filthy, cold, rat-ridden dressing room by day and a single room in a cheap boardinghouse at night. But working in vaudeville offered a remarkable level of independence in an era when women did nothing alone, not even walk down the street. Sophie made her own decisions about what to sing, how to sing, and what to wear. Later she recorded a song that expressed her satisfaction: "I do what I choose, whenever I choose / I go where I choose and take what I choose / And I'm not taking orders from no one."

Except in matters of makeup. Every time she asked the booking agent if she could work in whiteface, the same answer came back: "No. Blackface is what we want." She resented having to wear a disguise but accepted it as part of her training. "I never liked it, but I stumbled into the discovery that I could do it and that people liked it."

The critics liked it right away. "Seldom is such a vivacious, intense and entertaining personality found in one body," said an early review in the *New York Dramatic Mirror*. "Miss Tucker fairly lifts a person out of his seat. She has a very powerful voice of the 'coon shouting' caliber, but which she uses to such good advantage that the harshness of it is forgotten and her higher and lower notes are quite pleasing. But it isn't her voice. It's her ability to act. . . ."

Arriving for a show in Boston in 1908, Sophie got bad news: Her trunk had been sent on to another town by mistake, and inside it was her entire blackface getup—the black greasepaint, gloves, and horsehair wig. Posters announcing SOPHIE TUCKER: WORLD-RENOWNED COON SHOUTER were plastered all over the city. What was she going to do? The theater manager was unperturbed. "Go on in your street clothes, the way you are. A good-looking hefty squaw like you don't need black makeup."

Encouraging words. But Sophie was terrified. She had never walked out onstage without some kind of disguise, and here she was in a skirt suit, white blouse, and no makeup except lipstick, a dab of rouge, and a dusting of white powder. "You-all can see I'm a white girl," she began. "Well, I'll tell you something more: I'm not Southern. I'm a Jewish girl, and I just learned this Southern accent doing a blackface act for two years. And now, Mr. Leader, please play my song." She started with "That Lovin' Rag," and the audience was attentive. All the while she was thinking, "I don't need blackface. I can hold an audience without it. I've got them eating out of my hand."

When the trunk finally arrived in Boston, the theater manager intercepted it on its way to Sophie's dressing room. "Throw out that trunk," he said. "The kid doesn't need blackface." Sophie was free.

Two years later, in 1910, she made her entry into big-time vaudeville, where she did just two shows a day instead of the usual three or four and more, up to fourteen. Big time also meant big money, but not immediately. While Pauline, a famous hypnotist, was raking in $4,000 a week, and the equally well-known Julian Eltinge, a man impersonating a woman, was making $3,500, Sophie started out at $40. She gave her work everything

When West Twenty-eighth Street Was the Noisiest Street in New York

Although recordings of popular music existed in the early part of the century, they were relatively few. For the most part, if people wanted to hear popular songs, they bought sheet music for a quarter, played the music on the piano, and sang the lyrics.

The source for sheet music was West Twenty-eighth Street, where nearly all of the music publishers in the country had their offices. The street was known as Tin Pan Alley because of the din issuing from the windows and doorways as pianists thumped out the latest tunes for customers.

Vaudeville singers like Sophie Tucker were big customers on Twenty-eighth Street. They needed a constant supply of new songs, and in Tin Pan Alley they found piano players ready to run through the latest compositions for them, and arrangers available to make custom arrangements on the spot.

The music publishers, in turn, courted the better known singers, sending "song pluggers" to greet them at the theater, buy their meals, pay their hotel bills, hire taxicabs for them—anything to get a singer to try out a new song. If she did, then the publisher put her photograph on the sheet music cover, which helped sell the song to people who had liked it in the theater. Sophie frequently saw her likeness on sheet music.

she had, and her salary increased to $75 by the second week, then jumped to $100. The critics commented cruelly on her size—"speaking of elephants and ladies, there is Sophie Tucker"—but it was clear she was holding her own in big time. *Variety*, the national newspaper for theater, and other publications wrote of her "magnetism." In the *Chicago News*, a critic gushed: "She is a perfect cyclone of animation and makes such a terrific racket while singing and talks so loud and urges natural-born laughter to such extremes that her vitality is a tonic and a treat."

That same year, Sophie saw her name in lights. She took a picture of the marquee in Atlantic City, New Jersey, with her Brownie camera, and cried. She was a headliner at last.

"There's no getting round it, success does things to you," she said. "Makes you feel different, act different. I was strutting now." For the first time in her life she did not have to worry about money. Her salary went to $500 a week in 1911, when the average worker earned $750 a *year*. She sent money regularly to her parents and to Anna, who was raising Bert; paid Bert's private school tuition; put her brother through law school; and made a down payment on a house in Hartford for her parents—and still had cash to spare.

Sophie developed a taste for finery, the showier the better. She had four rings made of bright green stones to enhance the performance of one song, "Angle-worm Wiggle." She slid her hands up and down her body, hoping for a naughty effect, and she was not disappointed. In Portland, Oregon, the City Department of Safety for Women tried to have her arrested. She left the show while the authorities straightened out the matter. When the district attorney read the song's lyrics, he threw out the case. Sophie went back into the show, only now with a line at the box office that was three blocks long.

Sophie had a strong, unfailing sense of good business. Before she left each theater, she asked the manager for a return date, promising new songs. Unlike some vaudevillians, who kept the same act for several seasons, she changed her act frequently. One who shared her philosophy was the great blackface comedian Bert Williams, a black man, who mused, "If I could turn myself into a human boomerang; if I could jump from the stage, fly out over the audience, turn a couple of somersaults in the air,

The great blackface comedian Bert Williams: "always finding something new."

snatch the toupee from the head of the bald man in the front row of the balcony, and light back on the stage in the spot I jumped from, I could have the world at my feet—for a while. But even then I would always have to be finding something new."

For Sophie, "new" meant new songs from the "boys" in Tin Pan Alley, new clothes, new photos for the publicity men, new props. She sailed to London in 1922 and was a success there, but returned penniless because she spent everything she earned on gorgeous gowns and a one-thousand-dollar stage setting: black patent-leather drops that turned all colors when the lights hit them.

Sophie used her business sense in other ways, too. In contrast to her contemporary Eva Tanguay, who once tossed a stagehand down the stairs when he got in her way, Sophie made it a rule never to fuss backstage. She gave monetary tips to the stage crews and orchestra leaders, so that when she came back to their theaters, she'd have friends who would help her to be a success. She kept a file of seven thousand names of people she'd met over the years, and sent each of them a handwritten note when she was appearing in their community.

Being a good businesswoman paid off. Sophie earned top fees by the late 1920s, $3,500 and more per week. She performed for the king and queen of England, and in Paris, where she earned an astounding $7,000 a week.

She easily could afford to throw a grand wedding party for Anna when her sister got married in 1928. Otherwise Sophie found it difficult to maintain much of a family life. She stayed in touch with her son, but their relationship was always troubled. She married three times, briefly and without much happiness. Her felicity lay elsewhere. "I have just two passions in life," she said in 1913. "One is a fifty-horsepower go-as-you-please automobile and the other is a ragtime song with about the same amount of speed behind it."

WHAT SOPHIE WORE

★ Diamonds. Vaudevillians were great accumulators of diamond jewelry. If they were short of money, they could always take a diamond ring into a pawnshop and trade it for cash on the spot. Sophie kept her jewels in a pouch strapped around her waist under her costume so they wouldn't be stolen from her dressing room while she was onstage. For her triumphal return to her hometown of Hartford, Connecticut, as a headliner in 1913, Sophie wore a gown of white satin with a big black bow in front, a black lace skullcap, and all her diamond rings and necklaces.

★ Sophie went into debt to buy a leopard-skin coat trimmed in sealskin, a matching sealskin muff, and a hat with a leopard-skin bow. "*I sure was a loud baby. You could see me coming five blocks off.*" When she discovered the other actors didn't want to go out with her in such clothes, she traded the coat for one made of plain sealskin.

★ Sophie wore a very tight sheath skirt with a side slit to the knee, which was "*very, very daring in those days*" (1911), also very, very good for business. When she took a stroll down Main Street in Youngstown, Ohio, a crowd followed her back to the theater.

★ For a performance for the king and queen of England in 1934, Sophie chose a lovely white lace ensemble with coral and diamond jewelry. Fiddling with her bracelet as she sang, she caused the coral balls to drop off. By the end of her first song, she was slipping on the balls. When she tried to curtsy, her heel got caught in the lace of her skirt. She gave a salute, and the royals howled with laughter.

★ When Sophie started out performing, she, like many singers, didn't know what to do with her hands. She came up with the idea of a white handkerchief, which she could pull on and flutter, to keep her nervous hands occupied. "*It helped me, and as it became identified with me ('here's Sophie and her hanky'), I always carried one.*"

   "*In show business clothes matter. This was proved to me at the first matinee I went to at Hammerstein's [theater] in New York, when I heard the women seated near me commenting more on what the performers wore than on what they did. You had to please the women patrons to be and stay a headliner.*"

★ Clothes mattered to critics of vaudeville, too. "Sophie enhanced her physical charms by a gorgeous blue-gray gown and a stunning picture hat, with gorgeous feather trimmings for both," praised a reviewer in the *New York Telegraph* in 1911.

The Palace Theatre on Forty-seventh Street and Broadway, New York City, where Sophie Tucker was paid three thousand dollars a week to perform in 1927. When Ethel Merman was a child, her parents took her to see vaudeville at the Palace every Friday night. Judy Garland and Bette Midler also "played the Palace" in 1951 and 1978, respectively.

(BILLY ROSE THEATRE COLLECTION, THE NEW YORK PUBLIC LIBRARY FOR THE PERFORMING ARTS, ASTOR, LENOX AND TILDEN FOUNDATIONS)

Her most famous song, "Some of These Days," is hardly a powerhouse, at least on paper. The lyrics are rather bland: "Some of these days, you'll miss me honey / Some of these days, you'll feel so lonely / You'll miss my hugging, you'll miss my kissing / You'll miss me honey when you go away." It was Sophie's vigor that transformed the song into a showpiece. On TV in 1957, when Sophie was seventy, she sang the song to a Dixieland beat, fast and cocky, swirling her frothy skirt, flashing surprisingly slender calves, waving a chiffon scarf: "You're gonna miss your big fat momma some of these days."

Another favorite song was a sentimental number, "My Yiddishe Mama," sung in English and in Yiddish: "I need her more than ever now, my Yiddishe mama, I'd love to kiss that wrinkled brow." Sophie sang bawdy, seductive songs, too, about how she could "make a bald headed man part his hair in the middle" because she was "a red hot mama." With that song, introduced in 1928, she got the billing and nickname that stayed with her for the rest of her life: "The Last of the Red-hot Mamas."

Sadly, by then vaudeville was beginning its decline. Talking movies arrived in the late 1920s, and although many theaters offered a combination movie-and-vaudeville show, it was clear that audiences came to see the movie, not the live show. Vaudevillians got to be known as "coolers" because they stayed onstage only as long as the movie projectors needed to cool down. Sophie eventually accepted a pay cut and let her headliner status go to a movie actress, just to keep working. "Show business is changing all the time. If you want to stay with it, you have to change with it," she said.

As movies got longer, the vaudeville portion of the show shortened until it vanished altogether. Some vaudevillians went to Hollywood in the 1930s, but many abandoned the entertainment business altogether. Sophie kept working. She made six films, of which *Broadway Melody of 1938*, where she played Judy Garland's mother, was probably the best. Sophie needed a live audience, and did her best work in nightclubs. Her classy club act was the talk of the town for two more decades. She walked around the room and bantered with individuals in the crowd, spreading humor and goodwill like confetti. It didn't hurt that she wore outrageously expensive gowns and kept up a steady supply of new songs.

Sophie never retired. Before she died on February 10, 1966, at the age of seventy-nine, Sophie summed up her career in a few words: "God has been very good to me. He gave me special things that I took advantage of— I didn't sit around and let anybody beat me to the punch."

Answering mail at age sixty-five, Sophie Tucker kept track of almost everyone she had ever met. In her later life, she sent some five thousand Christmas cards a year.
(LIBRARY OF CONGRESS)

Madame Gertrude Rainey.
(FRANK DRIGGS COLLECTION)

MA RAINEY

Mother of the Blues

BADIN, NORTH CAROLINA, didn't have much in the way of entertainment in 1917. There was just one theater, where audiences could see silent movies like *The Immigrant* with Charlie Chaplin, a comedy act, and perhaps a dog doing tricks. Imagine the excitement when Ma Rainey and the Georgia Smart Set, a black minstrel troupe, arrived that June, set up a two-hundred-foot-long tent, and put on a two-hour show. Clyde Bernhardt, a boy who became a jazz trombone player, went to see the performance every night for several weeks. Inside the segregated tent, blacks sat on one side, whites sat on the other. The curtain opened, and out pranced eight black women in short costumes, dancing fast. Comedians told funny stories, and a man pedaled a bicycle every which way, sitting, standing, on his head, on his back, all the while holding an umbrella. A juggler put two lighted oil lamps on his head, turned around and upside down, and did a back flip, without extinguishing a flame.

Madame Gertrude Rainey came onstage last. "The great lady started singing in the wings and as the curtains opened, strutted out flashing those gold-plated teeth and her expensive gold necklace," Clyde Bernhardt wrote. "She wore a long, gold silk gown that swept along the floor, gold slippers, and carried a sparkling rhinestone walking cane. Her hat was high and wide with large feathers stuck in it, had gold earrings dangling and diamond rings on all her fingers. When she got to center stage under those amber spotlights, the audience just went wild."

"Ma" Rainey, as she was called, was a minstrel-show performer: a singer, dancer, and comedienne. She was most famous for the tent shows she set up in small towns all over the South, although she also worked in theaters in big cities in the North and South. The tent shows traveled by train, in their own railroad cars—blacks weren't allowed to ride with whites in the same car, and the "colored only" car was already crowded, so traveling companies with more than twenty-five performers purchased their own cars. The companies had colorful names like King and Bush Wide-Mouth Minstrels, Florida Cotton Blossoms, Shufflin' Sam from Alabam', and the two most famous: Silas Green from New Orleans and the Rabbit Foot Minstrels. When the "Foots," of which Ma was at one time a member, came to town, a band marched up and down the streets, playing music to advertise the show. The Foots played one-night stands, so they were an especially portable troupe. Their tent was relatively small, 80 by 110 feet, and the stage was made of boards laid across a folding frame. Coleman lanterns served as footlights, and there were no microphones. Some of the weaker-voiced women used megaphones, but not Ma. She had developed enough vocal projection to make the songs "Florida Blues," "Kansas City Blues," and "Walking the Dog" heard *outside* her tent.

Ma was, by all accounts, a fabulous performer. Short and heavyset, she had a wide nose, big lips, and a mouth full of gold-capped teeth. She was not refined looking, but she had something that drew people to her. "She wouldn't have to sing any words; she would moan, and the audience would moan with her," the poet Sterling Brown recalled.

It is not known how or where Ma learned to sing and dance. Gertrude Rainey was born on April 26, 1886, in Columbus, Georgia. Her father died when she was ten years old, and her mother went to work for the railroad to support Gertrude and her four siblings. When she was fourteen, Gertrude made her professional debut in a musical revue, A Bunch of Blackberries, in Columbus.

Any black girl would have found the traveling shows enticing, with their promise of glamour and wealth, or at the very least, a more interesting life than that of a laundress, cook, or maid—the usual occupations for black

American women at the turn of the twentieth century. Gertrude was enticed *and* talented: When a minstrel show came through town in 1904, she married one of the performers, a dancer, comedian, and singer named William Rainey, and they became a song-and-dance team, traveling with various troupes. She was eighteen.

Gertrude entered a complicated business. Black-minstrel shows grew out of the white-minstrel shows, which originated the practice, now seen as racist, of blackening people's faces with burnt cork and outlining their lips in white greasepaint to make them look like black slaves. These "blackface minstrels" put on skits about plantation life. They strummed banjos, rolled their eyes and grinned, and did odd little dances. One of the songs they sang, "Weel about and turn about and do jus so / ebery time I weel about, I jump Jim Crow," gave rise to the expression "Jim Crow," which came to symbolize discrimination against blacks.

After slaves were emancipated in 1863, blacks adopted the white-minstrel routines, and even blackened their faces, but they advertised themselves as "authentic Negroes." Billy Kersands was one of the best-known black minstrels; a comic and a dancer, Billy could put a whole coffee cup and saucer in his mouth. Black-minstrel shows appealed to whites and blacks. Whites enjoyed watching "real Negroes" acting as whites expected they should, ignorant and amusing, while blacks laughed to see other blacks making fun of the white blackface tradition. Blackface comedy eventually became a part of vaudeville, where Sophie Tucker was told to "black up" if she wanted a job.

By the time Gertrude joined the minstrel

What's New?

Silent Films Grow Up

Most silent movies were crude, ten- or fifteen-minute entertainments until *The Birth of a Nation,* in 1915. The movie cost one hundred thousand dollars to make and lasted more than three hours. The moving picture industry's first epic portrayed Northern and Southern families in Civil War times, and painted Negroes as villains and the men in the Ku Klux Klan as heroes. The newly formed National Association for the Advancement of Colored People (NAACP) led demonstrations against the movie, which eventually was banned in five states and nineteen cities.

In 1916, the first movie star, Charlie Chaplin, signed a contract for twelve movies, to be made in one year, for $675,000. The average salary in America was $750 a year. Chaplin's best-known movies are *The Great Dictator, Modern Times, The Pawnshop,* and *The Kid.*

Thirty million people in America went to the movies in a week (just 6.8 million went to baseball games). Admission was five to ten cents on average, but two dollars for "specials" like *The Birth of a Nation.*

Microphone

The first crystal microphone, with high-quality sound, was produced in 1919.

life, black minstrelsy had become a kind of elaborate variety show, not unlike a circus, with singers, acrobats, jugglers, comedians, dancers, and musicians as well as the occasional snake charmer—all for as little as thirty cents.

William Rainey's nickname was Pa, so Gertrude quickly became Ma. From 1914 to 1916 the young couple toured with Tolliver's Circus and Musical Extravaganza, billed as "Rainey and Rainey, Assassinators of the Blues." Soon Ma began heading shows of her own. Sometime in the late teens the couple separated, and Pa died, but she always remained Ma Rainey.

Audiences took to her immediately, in a visceral way. One night in New Orleans around 1914 she sang, "If you don't believe I'm sinkin', look what a hole I'm in," and the stage collapsed—by accident. She wasn't hurt, and everybody had a good laugh.

Ma Rainey and her Wildcats Jazz Band, in 1923.
(DUNCAN SCHEIDT COLLECTION)

Ma had a rare ability to communicate deeply with ordinary people, Southerners in particular. "Bessie [Smith] was the greater blues singer, but Ma really *knew* these people; she was a person of the folk; she was very simple and direct," said Sterling Brown. In his poem "Ma Rainey," he wrote: "I talked to a fellow, an' the fellow say, 'She jes' catch hold of us, somekindaway.'"

Ma was also sweet-tempered, warm, and clean spoken. "She didn't put on no airs, or nothin' like that; she never did use no bad language," remembered Clyde Bernhardt. When she came to Badin, North Carolina, his hometown, in 1917, Clyde brought her bottles of her favorite drink, Coca-Cola, sat with her, and watched as she put on her makeup. Ma was dark-skinned at a time when the bias among whites and blacks alike was toward lighter-skinned black people, so she put on greasepaint, powder, and rouge to make her skin look more pale. "Honey, it's hard work to be light like me. Takes a hour to put that makeup on and another to get the damn stuff off," she told the entranced young Clyde.

Ma was a generous woman: When a new musician joined her band, she bought an instrument for him or her (at one time Ma's band had a female member, unusual for the time, cornetist Doll Jones). "She had a heart as big as [a] house," said Artiebelle McGinty, a younger singing, dancing comedienne who performed with Ma.

While Ma was becoming a star of the minstrel-show circuit, a singer named Mamie Smith achieved fame overnight with the first blues record. In 1920 Mamie's "Crazy Blues" record sold seventy-five thousand copies in its first month, prompting a mad scramble among record companies to find other women who could sing the blues. Surprisingly, record producers did not go immediately to Ma Rainey, despite the fact that she had been singing the blues since 1902. A possible reason might be that Ma was based in Chicago, and most of the producers were in New York. In any event, Clara Smith, Bessie Smith (no relation to each other or to Mamie), and Ida Cox all made records before Ma. Finally, in December of 1923, Paramount Records of Chicago approached Ma and signed a contract. "Honey, I thought they overlooked this old lady. But I had faith in the Lord," she told Clyde. She was thirty-seven years old.

DISCOVERED AT LAST—MA RAINEY, MOTHER OF THE BLUES read Paramount's ad in the *Chicago Defender* newspaper, although this was not news to Ma's many fans in the South. Ma's second career, as a recording artist and blues singer, was underway, and she made the most of it, recording at least ninety-two songs in five years. As soon as her records started selling, she began doing tours set up by the Theater Owners' Booking Agency (TOBA), a circuit of more than fifty theaters in the South and Midwest featuring black entertainment. The joke among the performers was that TOBA stood for "Tough on Black Actors" because the agency exploited performers by giving them a grueling schedule and low compensation. "At that time on TOBA you *work*—you do five, six shows a day; you got little money, but everybody was happy," said Lonnie Johnson, a blues singer.

It certainly was a happy time for Ma Rainey. Her pianist and the band director of her Wild Cats Jazz Band, Thomas Dorsey, recalled their debut at Chicago's Grand Theater in April 1924: "I shall never forget the excited feeling when the orchestra in the pit struck up her opening theme, music which I had written especially for the show. The curtain rose slowly and those soft lights on the band as we picked up the introduction to Ma's first song. We looked and felt like a million. Ma was hidden in a big box-like affair built like an old Victrola of long ago. . . . A girl would come out and put a big record on it. Then the band picked up the 'Moonshine Blues.' Ma would sing a few bars inside the Victrola. Then she would open the door and step out into the spotlight with her glittering gown that weighed twenty pounds and wearing a necklace of five, ten and twenty dollar gold pieces. The house went wild . . . Ma had the audience in the palm of her hand." They took seven curtain calls that night.

WHAT MA WORE

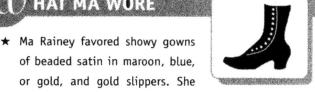

★ Ma Rainey favored showy gowns of beaded satin in maroon, blue, or gold, and gold slippers. She also often wore a sequined black dress with shiny black pointed-toe slippers. Two of her trademarks were a fan of ostrich plumes, and a rhinestone-studded cane, which she used even as a young woman.

★ Ma was uncommonly fond of jewelry, and wore diamond-studded tiaras, rings, and bracelets. She was most famous for a heavy necklace and matching earrings made of five-, ten-, and twenty-dollar gold coins, which she cleaned regularly with Old Dutch Cleanser.

By 1926 Ma was touring in a seven-person limousine, and the following year she did well enough, combining tent shows and TOBA performances, to buy a thirteen thousand-dollar Mack bus emblazoned with her name.

Although she never achieved the fame of fellow blues singer and recording artist Bessie Smith, her records sold well (mostly by mail, for seventy-five cents each). Bessie sang better than Ma, more on pitch, with slightly better diction and more control of tone, and her recording company, Columbia, put out a better product than Paramount. Ma Rainey's records, some of which have been remastered for compact disc, were noisy and blurry. Her diction was so poor, it's sometimes impossible to hear the words. She had a deep, dark voice. It was forceful and seemed to come with effort, which gave a certain weight to the lyrics.

Ma sang mostly about losing a man. Although she lived in a time of terrible racial prejudice, of lynchings and riots, she didn't sing about those things. "What's the use of living if you can't get the man you love?" she wails in "Bad Luck Blues." "You might as well go die and give your soul to the Maker above."

The first newspaper advertisement for Ma Rainey's recordings, in the *Chicago Defender*, a newspaper for African Americans, in 1924.

(PHOTOGRAPHS AND PRINTS DIVISION, SCHOMBERG CENTER FOR RESEARCH IN BLACK CULTURE, THE NEW YORK PUBLIC LIBRARY, ASTOR, LENOX AND TILDEN FOUNDATIONS)

Within the advertisement:

"Jealous Hearted Blues"
Sung by "Ma" Rainey

"You can have my money, everything I own
But please just leave my man alone,
Cuz I'm jealous, jealous,
I'm jealous as I can be."

IT takes "Ma" Rainey—the Mother of the Blues—to sing a hit like this. Hear her tell the shebas to leave her man alone—hear about what she's gonna do with a bull-dog if her man don't quit foolin' 'round. Be sure to get Paramount No. 12252. On the other side is another corker by "Ma"—"See See Rider Blues".

You Can't Go Wrong With These

12246—Drunk Man's Strut and Red Hot Mama. Jimmie O'Bryant and his sensational Washboard Band. Hear the wicked moaning clarinet and the washboard harmony.

12241—Barnum's Steam Calliope and Didn't He Ramble, great novelty record by Sunset Four.

12098—Dream Blues and Lost Wandering Blues, "Ma" Rainey's great Souvenir Record. Her picture right on the record. No extra charge.

12282—Jealous Hearted Blues and See See Rider Blues. "Ma" Rainey and her Georgia Jazz Band.

12236—Salty Dog Blues and Salt Lake City Blues, "Papa" Charley Jackson.

12243—Down By the River Blues and Don't Dog Me 'Round, Sodarisa Miller.

12245—Choo Choo Blues and Ride Jockey Ride, Trixie Smith and Her Down Home Syncopators.

12242—Booze and Blues and Toad Frog Blues, "Ma" Rainey.

20364—Big Fat Mama Blues and Gin House Blues, Clarinet solos by Boyd Senter.

12247—West Indies Blues and Go Long Mule, by Ukulele "Bob" Williams.

12240—Delta Bottom Blues and I Never Call My Man's Name, Priscilla Stewart.

12226—Cherry Picking Blues and Wild Women Don't Have No Blues, Ida Cox.

Race's Favorite Spirituals

12035—Father Prepare Me and My Lord's Gonna Move this Wicked Race, Norfolk Jubilee Quartette.

12073—When All The Saints Come Marching in and That Old-Time Religion, Paramount Jubilee Singers.

12217—Ezekiel Saw De Wheel and Crying Holy Unto The Lord, Norfolk Jubilee Quartette.

12234—Where Shall I Be and I'm Gonna Build Right on Dat Shore, Norfolk Jubilee Quartette.

Send No Money! If your dealer hasn't the Paramount records you want, just check them on the coupon at the right and mail to us. Pay postman when he brings the records to your door. 75 cents each, plus 10-cent C. O. D. fee. We pay postage and insurance.

THE NEW YORK RECORDING LABORATORIES

Paramount
[Including Black Swan]
The Popular Race Record

Paramount Records promoted a new Ma Rainey recording, "Jealous Hearted Blues," in the *Chicago Defender*, 1925.

(PHOTOGRAPHS AND PRINTS DIVISION, SCHOMBERG CENTER FOR RESEARCH IN BLACK CULTURE, THE NEW YORK PUBLIC LIBRARY, ASTOR, LENOX AND TILDEN FOUNDATIONS)

In the songs Ma chose, women were routinely beaten and otherwise mistreated by their men. In "Weepin' Woman Blues," she wishes for death by drowning: "I'd rather be in the river, driftin' like a log/ Than to be in this town, treated like a dog." Rage runs through many of the songs, and violence leads to more violence, even murder. In "Cell Band Blues," the singer tells her jailer how she hadn't wanted to kill her lover, but he hit her and: "First shot I fired, my man fell dead."

It's hard to imagine a woman who was called "gracious" and "compassionate" singing about such violence. But her recording repertoire was driven to some extent by public demand, a demand that had been created by other singers who had recorded such songs. Even if she didn't live a violent life, Ma was a gifted singing actress who was able to portray experiences outside her own. On the other hand, thirty-eight of the ninety-two recorded songs are her own compositions, and some of the songs are considered to be autobiographical. In "Bo-Weevil Blues," one of her biggest hits, the singer boasts how she avoids men because "Some of them's so evil, I'm afraid they might poison me." But later in the song, the singer buys a new hat and sadly puts it on the shelf, realizing how lonely she is.

Ma was probably bisexual. She favored younger men, but she also got arrested once for running an indecent party with her chorus girls, and she may have had an intimate relationship with Bessie Smith. Ma also wrote a song about lesbianism, "Prove It on Me Blues," in which she defies anyone to prove she is a lesbian—or "crooked," as she called it, but leaves broad hints as to her sexual preference: "Went out last night with a crowd of my friends/They must've been women, 'cause I don't like no men."

Not all of Ma's songs were so weighty in their subject matter. In "Those Dogs of Mine," she sang about the corns on her feet ("dogs").

Ma Rainey's recording career came to a sudden end in 1928, when Paramount dropped her from its list. "Her down-home material had gone out of fashion," a recording executive explained. In fact, black show business in general was in a demise. TOBA shows declined in quality, and ceased altogether after the stock market crash of 1929. Talking movies and radio shows were the rage, and people no longer wanted to spend their leisure time at live shows.

But Ma wasn't done yet. She continued performing in minstrel shows in the South, where people still enjoyed the old-time entertainment. Work was scarcer than before, and she sometimes had to settle for carnivals and livestock shows. She sold her personalized bus and traveled in a house trailer made out of an old car. Instead of the famous gold-coin necklace, which she probably sold, Ma wore imitation pearls.

In 1935 she retired to Columbus, Georgia, where she had built a home. Some years back she had purchased two theaters in Rome, Georgia, the Lyric and the Airdome, and continued to operate them. She joined the church where her brother Thomas Pridgett, Jr., was a deacon. On December 22, 1939, Ma died quietly at the age of fifty-three of heart disease, and was buried without fanfare in the family plot in Columbus. Just four short years of retirement had extinguished her celebrity. On her death certificate, the coroner listed her occupation as "housekeeping." He was obviously unacquainted with the "Mother of the Blues," unaware that Gertrude Rainey had been, as historian Charles Edward Smith noted later, "the voice of the South, singing of the South, to the South."

Bessie Smith
liked elaborate
clothes, and
especially head
wear, in the
1920s. This
photo is signed,
"To Palamida, my
gown designer."

BESSIE SMITH

Empress of the Blues

B
ESSIE SMITH was twenty-eight years old when she entered a recording studio for the first time on February 15, 1923. She was wearing a new dress, a gift from her boyfriend, Jack Gee, who had pawned his night watchman's uniform and his pocket watch to buy it. Bessie faced a large cone-shaped horn that protruded from a drapery-covered wall, as this was a time before microphones. The engineer stood behind the wall, peering into the studio from a small window. His job was to watch as a stylus picked up vibrations from the horn and cut a groove in a revolving wax disc—the master from which a record would be pressed.

Recording technology was in its infancy, so there was no editing, no listening to playbacks. Bessie and her piano player, Clarence Williams, simply had to perform a number over and over until the Columbia Records producer, Frank Walker, announced a successful "take."

Bessie must have been nervous: She sang the first song, "'Tain't Nobody's Bizness If I Do," nine times, and the second, "Down Hearted Blues," twice, whereupon the producer told everybody to go home and come back the following day.

The next day, on the third take of "Down Hearted Blues," Clarence Williams played the short introduction in steady, if rather plodding, ragtime. Bessie came in a little tentatively, singing, "Gee, but it's hard to love someone when that someone don't love *yooo*," and gained confidence as

The Blues Aren't Always Blue

The blues is a kind of black American folk music that takes the form of a song or an instrumental piece, often for guitar or piano and, most important, the blues is personal. Whereas a popular song might relate the story of "the doggie in the window" or "some enchanted evening," a blues song is about the singer's (or songwriter's) own experiences.

Usually the personal experience involves trouble of one sort or another: lost love, crime, imprisonment, alcohol, natural disasters. There are humorous blues songs, however, such as "Sorrowful Blues," in which Bessie sings about having nineteen men and wanting just one more. And there are occasional songs about social protest, like "Poor Man's Blues," which Bessie wrote, asking a rich man to give to a poor man in hard times.

The blues were originally sung by ex-slaves struggling to eke out a living after Emancipation, but the feelings expressed—anger, fear, despair, and occasional joy—are timeless and universal. People continue to listen to the blues because when they hear someone else express the feelings that they have, even dark, gloomy feelings, they generally feel a little better. Or, as songwriter W. C. Handy said, "The blues came from nothingness, from want, from desire. And when [someone] sang or played the blues, a small part of the want was satisfied from the music."

the song went on. By the time she got to "Trouble, trouble, I've had it all my days," she was singing full out, her voice strong and sure.

Walker pronounced the third take "satisfactory"; he did the same with the song on the flip side, "Gulf Coast Blues." (A 78 rpm record had one song to each side. A singer got paid only for the sides that were pronounced satisfactory, not the rejects.)

Bessie's record sold 780,000 copies in just six months. She would become the highest-paid black entertainer of her time, and rightly deserve the title "Empress of the Blues."

Bessie was not, however, the first to sing the blues on recording. Mamie Smith, no relation to Bessie, got there first, in 1920. Mamie used an all-black band as accompaniment—a daring move at the time, since only white bands were recording the new music called "jazz." "Crazy Blues," by "Mamie Smith and Her Jazz Hounds," was a phenomenally successful record that launched the boom in blues singing and started a whole new industry called "race records"—recordings made by and for blacks.

Although the term "race records" may sound derogatory today, in the 1920s, it was acceptable, even appealing, to blacks. "Race" was an expression of pride; blacks referred to themselves as the Negro race, or "the race," for short, implying a sense of brotherhood. When records by lady blues singers started selling, record companies were quick to pair the word "race" with "records" as a way of appealing to black consumers. Most, but not all, of the race records were by female blues singers.

The success of Mamie's "Crazy Blues" made the recording industry pay attention to the Negro market for the first time. Previously the record business had assumed that blacks couldn't afford phonographs. Not only could "the race" come up with the money for phonographs—$28.95 for a Silvertone windup "Ideal" model from Sears—but it eagerly purchased records, at seventy-five cents apiece, as fast as the companies could make them. When whites discovered the music, they, too, eagerly bought race records, particularly Bessie's.

If she was powerful on recording, "Miss Bessie" was positively mesmerizing in person. Standing five feet nine inches tall and weighing about two hundred pounds, Bessie walked with the stately grace of a queen. Her eyes shone, and she flashed a bright smile.

"Bessie was a real woman, all woman, all the femaleness the world ever saw in one sweet package," said Mezz Mezzrow, a friend, clarinetist, and saxophonist from Chicago. "She was tall and brown-skinned, with great big dimples creasing her cheeks, dripping good looks—just this side of voluptuous, buxom and massive, but stately, too, shapely as a hourglass, with a high-voltage magnet for a personality."

Bessie was born in 1894 and grew up terribly poor in what she described as a "little ramshackle cabin" in Chattanooga, Tennessee. By the time she was nine years old, her father—a laborer and part-time Baptist preacher—and her mother and a brother were dead (probably from illness and lack of medical care, although the reasons are unknown), leaving Bessie's oldest sister, Viola, in charge of five children.

Being poor and black in the South, the Smith children had little future. Black girls generally grew up to be maids or laundresses,

Bessie Smith in 1936, in a photograph taken by Carl Van Vechten, a white photographer and writer who helped introduce Bessie to white audiences. He wrote: "Her face was beautiful, with the rich, ripe beauty of southern darkness. . . ."
(LIBRARY OF CONGRESS)

or they cared for white people's children. Black boys became laborers. But if a black child had talent, he or she could join one of the traveling shows and become an entertainer, just as Ma Rainey had done in 1904.

Bessie got her start singing and dancing on the streets for pennies and nickels. She had nine years' experience when her older brother, Clarence, joined a traveling show as a dancer and a comedian, and arranged an audition for his sister. The Moses Stokes Minstrel Troupe hired Bessie, primarily as a dancer. She was eighteen.

A theater manager saw Bessie perform a year later and offered this description: "She didn't know how to dress—she just sang in her street clothes—but she was such a natural that she could wreck anybody's show. She only made ten dollars a week, but people would throw money on the stage, and the stage hands would pick up about three or four dollars for her after every performance, especially when she sang the 'Weary Blues.'"

Bessie joined the black vaudeville circuit organized by the Theater Owners' Booking Agency (TOBA), singing her blues in a diverse variety show of as many as twenty acts. In 1918 the bill at the Douglas Gilmor Theatre in Baltimore, for example, featured: "Ralph Harris & Alda Fatima In their Latest 'Who is Who'; Holmes & Edwards, The Crazy Man and the Maid; Hazel Green & Bessie Smith, Hip Ha Hip Ha Girls—Men here is a chance for a Good Wife; Special Feature Pictures Changed Daily—

WHAT BESSIE WORE

★ Bessie wore Evening in Paris perfume. She wore horsehair wigs, straight or wavy, in the twenties; she pulled her own hair straight back in a bun in the thirties. She favored very little jewelry: bauble earrings; sometimes a strand of pearls.

★ Onstage she wore a white and blue satin dress, with hoop skirt, decorated with strands of pearls and fake rubies, and a white fringed hat that looked like a cross between a football helmet and a lamp shade. Sometimes she preferred a white-fringed dress with a large shawl trimmed in long fringe, and a beaded skullcap with a huge white ostrich feather. She simplified her style in the thirties and donned a white satin V-neck evening gown with a small matching shawl.

★ For a night on the town she liked to wear a white ermine coat.

★ At home she padded around in a housecoat and slippers.
   "Bessie liked to dress well, and she liked for her men to dress well, so she'd buy expensive suits for Jack and she got herself some fur coats and jewelry—real diamonds. At home she was still the same old Bessie, slopping around in her slippers, her hair flying all over the place, and cooking up a lot of greasy food," recalled her niece Ruby Walker.

Showing all the Latest Serials [silent movies]." And all this happened in less than two hours.

When record companies began scrambling to find blues singers to match Mamie Smith's success, they did not turn immediately to Bessie. She auditioned for at least two record companies, which turned her down. One record executive said her voice was too rough. She didn't sound a bit like Mamie Smith, who had a high, girlish voice; Bessie's voice was low and growly, and so powerful that, when microphones came into regular use around 1926, she had no use for one. Though untrained, Bessie sang squarely on pitch, and with a precise control of tone. She mumbled a lot of her words, but that didn't seem to bother her listeners. As blues singer Alberta Hunter said, "even though [Bessie] was raucous and loud, she had a tear—no, not a tear, but there was a *misery* in what she did."

With the release of her first record, Bessie went from rags to riches almost overnight. That summer of 1923, her fee for live performances jumped from fifty dollars a week, plus tips, to three hundred fifty dollars a week. A year later, Bessie could get one thousand and two thousand dollars a week—at a time when a good pair of shoes cost three dollars. Bessie had to pay the cast—her act included a chorus of singer-dancers—and assistants out of her salary, but their earnings were tiny by comparison: A chorus girl, for example, got about fifteen dollars a week.

In addition, Bessie earned money from recording: one hundred fifty dollars per "satisfactory side." The fee was raised in 1924 to two hundred dollars. She recorded 160 sides in ten years. Had she received royalties—or additional fees based on the amount of records sold—she would have been a millionaire, but no blues singers at that time were paid royalties.

What did Bessie do with her sudden wealth? Like most of the blues singers who found themselves suddenly richer than they ever could have imagined, she spent it. Mamie Smith had bought three residences. Bessie bought furs and jewels, and for Jack Gee, now her husband, three hundred-dollar suits and a diamond ring that cost more than two thousand dollars. One day in 1924, she and Jack jumped off a train in Ohio and impulsively bought a new car so they could drive the rest of the way to their destination in Detroit.

Blacks were not permitted to stay in the same hotels as whites, and hotels for blacks were scarce, especially in the South, where Bessie took

What's New?

Phonograph

In the 1920s the windup phonograph playing two-sided records became the norm (previously, records had only one side). The first electrical recording, with a microphone, took place in 1925. Phonographs went electric soon after electrical recording was introduced.

Radio

The first radio sets consisted of several components that the owner assembled to make a receiver, and an ear tube for listening. In 1924 the cumbersome system was replaced by the "radio music box," which was a big hit with consumers. Radio threatened to replace the phonograph because the quality of sound reproduction was better, and the music was free. The first commercial radio station was WWJ in Detroit, established in 1920. By 1929, nearly seven hundred radio stations were operating in the United States, and radio had become a national obsession.

A boy plays a record on a windup gramophone (phonograph) in the South in the 1930s.
(LIBRARY OF CONGRESS)

Bessie's first radio broadcast took place in Atlanta, Georgia, in June 1923, the same month her first record was released.

Jukebox

The first coin-slot machine with electronic amplification and a multirecord changer was built in 1927. Dancing, or "jooking," to records was especially popular in the South, which gave the machine its name, jukebox. The boxes could be found in bars, restaurants and cafés, variety stores, bus stations, and even barbershops and beauty parlors.

"Talkies"

Talking pictures, or movies, replaced silent films and helped kill vaudeville in the 1920s. The first talking picture was produced in 1927 and was actually a "singie": *The Jazz Singer,* featuring Al Jolson, the dancer and singer. The first real talkie was *Tenderloin,* an eighty-eight-minute film of which only fifteen minutes were dialogue, in 1928. By 1929, more than eight thousand sound-film theaters were operating in the United States.

Bessie made just one movie, the seventeen-minute *St. Louis Blues,* in 1929. In it, a guy named Jimmy throws her to the floor, kicks and robs her, and she ends up sitting in a bar, singing into her beer about her man with "a heart like a rock."

her tent show on annual tours. Bessie's biggest purchase, therefore, was her most practical. She bought a custom-made railroad car. Her sister-in-law, Maud Smith, recalled the day the railroad car was delivered to the troupe in a small Georgia town. "Everybody was so excited, and we laughed and carried on as we walked through the car and examined every corner. And what a difference it made—some of the towns we hit didn't have hotels for us, so we used to have to spread out, one staying here, another one there. Now we could just live on the train."

The bright yellow car was seventy-eight feet long and had seven staterooms that each slept four, a kitchen, a bathroom with hot and cold water, a lower level to accommodate thirty-five people, a storeroom for the big tent and the cases of soft drinks, Cracker Jack, and peanuts, and a corridor long enough to transport the tent's center pole. Bessie often did the cooking herself, working up a pot of pig's feet or stew for the musicians, chorus girls, prop boys—everybody.

Bessie shared her wealth, supporting her sisters and their children, and eventually buying a house for them near her own house, in Philadelphia. Her sisters responded with an act of generosity: When Bessie and Jack adopted a six-year-old boy, Jack Jr., in 1926, the sisters cared for him while Bessie was on the road, which was most of the time. Bessie also gave lots of money away, to anyone, strangers included, who needed it.

Generous as she was, Bessie was far from saintly. Although she showered her husband with expensive clothes and jewelry, she was frequently unfaithful to him (as he was unfaithful to her), and their fights often turned violent on both sides. Bessie had a terrible temper. If she caught a woman flirting with her husband or one of her lovers, it was nothing for Bessie to pull the woman's hair out and beat her, sometimes to the point of unconsciousness.

Bessie was especially ornery around white people. Unlike Ma Rainey, whose world was predominantly black people, Bessie, who was more famous, had plenty of contact with the white world. She performed at parties held by wealthy white people, for example. She was suspicious of their welcome, knowing full well that they would never permit a black elevator operator in their home, but they would invite her because she could entertain them. As she was leaving one party in New York, the white hostess stopped her. "Miss Smith," said the hostess, throwing her arms around Bessie's neck, "you're not leaving without kissing me good-bye!"

Bessie knocked the woman flat. She had been drinking great quantities of whiskey that evening, which probably fueled her temper. She was a binge drinker, and it got her into trouble more than once. In Wheeling, West Virginia, one night in 1931, Bessie went on a drinking binge and missed a performance. Roaming the unfamiliar streets, singing and cursing, she was arrested and thrown into jail. After a boyfriend bailed her out at 2 A.M., rather than apologize to her angry troupe, she packed up all the costumes and backdrops and departed at dawn in a rented truck. She left twenty-two performers and crew members, none of whom had been paid, without a cent and, of course, no job.

Yet, at times, she used her anger and aggression to positive effect. In the middle of a performance under a tent in North Carolina in 1927, one of the musicians discovered the Ku Klux Klan hanging around outside the tent, preparing to pull up the stakes and make the tent collapse on the show. When Bessie found out, she stormed up to the white-hooded and -sheeted men and, in a burst of profanity, told them to leave. At first the Klansmen were too surprised to move, but after Bessie hurled more obscenities at them, they turned and disappeared into the night.

"I ain't never *heard* of such shit," she said, using her favorite expression, and went back inside the tent to resume the show.

Making a big scene never caused Bessie much embarrassment, as long as it got her what she wanted. In 1936 Frank Schiffman, a theater owner in New York, refused to give her an advance against her salary. Bessie threw herself on the floor of the crowded theater lobby, kicking and hollering about how she was the star of the show and the owner wouldn't give her her money. Bessie got the advance.

Curiously, Schiffman had mostly kind words about Bessie. True, "she was a difficult and temperamental person," he said years later. "She had her love affairs, which frequently interfered with her work, but she never was a real problem. I don't remember any artist in all my long, long years—and this goes back to some of the famous singers, including Billie Holiday—who could evoke the response from her listeners that Bessie did. Whatever pathos there is in the world, whatever sadness she had, was brought out in her singing—and the audience knew it and responded to it."

One man who responded to Bessie's music was a photographer and writer named Carl Van Vechten, who took some friends to the Orpheum Theatre, in Newark, New Jersey, a slightly rundown establishment that catered to blacks and served as the city's showcase for top black entertainers. The theater had doubled its prices to one dollar, for Bessie's appearances during Thanksgiving week of 1925, and still the run was sold out.

Van Vechten described Bessie's performance in an article in *Vanity Fair* magazine, which had a primarily white readership: "As the curtain lifted, a jazz band, against a background of plum-colored hangings, held the full stage. The saxophone began to moan; the drummer tossed his sticks. . . . The hangings parted, and a great brown woman emerged . . . in a rose satin dress, spangled with sequins, which swept away from her trim ankles. Her face was beautiful, with the rich, ripe beauty of southern darkness, a deep bronze brown, like her bare arms.

"She walked slowly to the footlights.

"Then, to the accompaniment of the wailing, muted brasses, the monotonous African beat of the drum, the dromedary glide of the pianist's fingers over the responsive keys, she began her

Bessie Smith was forty-two when she posed for this Carl Van Vechten photograph.
(LIBRARY OF CONGRESS)

Dancing to the music on a jukebox in Clarksdale, Mississippi, 1939.
(LIBRARY OF CONGRESS)

strange rites in a voice full of shoutin' and moanin' and prayin' and sufferin,' a wild, rough Ethiopian voice, harsh and volcanic, released between rouged lips and the whitest of teeth, the singer swaying slightly to the rhythm."

The crowd, he wrote, "burst into hysterical shrieks of sorrow and lamentation."

Surely the Orpheum audience was responding to the "misery" in Bessie's voice and her stories. For Bessie told stories in song, and wrote many of the lyrics herself. She told stories about lost love: In "Weeping Willow Blues," she kisses her man and washes his clothes and tries to treat him right, but "now he's gone and left me after all I tried to do." She sang about independence: "If I should take a notion / To jump into the ocean /

'Tain't nobody's bizness if I do." And she flirted in song, asking her listeners if they'd ever seen peaches growing on a sweet potato vine, then beckoning to "take a peep at mine" ("Sorrowful Blues").

On one occasion, Bessie mourned about a public event, singing about a disastrous Mississippi River flood that rendered thousands homeless: "Back water blues done caused me to pack my things and go" ("Back Water Blues").

But the theme that recurred most in Bessie's songs was that of being abused by men, and loving them, anyway: "He blacked my eye, I couldn't see . . . But outside of that he's alright with me" ("Outside of That"). Bessie was familiar with such situations: Her husband, Jack, beat her, and eventually left her for another woman.

With the stock market crash in 1929 and the resulting Great Depression of the 1930s, the blues boom came to an end. People were out of work and couldn't scrape together forty-five cents for a pound of pork chops, let alone buy records—even when the price of a record dropped to thirty-five cents.

Columbia Records dropped Bessie from its roster in 1931 because her records were no longer selling. Still, Bessie managed to maintain a following, and continued to perform sporadically in theaters and nightclubs, primarily in Philadelphia, but also in New York City and the South.

When popular songs became the rage in the 1930s, Bessie willingly adjusted her repertoire. She sang "Smoke Gets in Your Eyes" and "Tea for Two," and in 1933, she made a record with the new-style swing-band accompaniment. Benny Goodman, the King of Swing, played clarinet on "Gimme a Pigfoot," a rowdy number about getting "full of corn [liquor]" and "bringin' 'em down [partying]."

Bessie was certainly on the verge of a second career as a popular singer, but tragically, her life was cut short. On the night of September 26, 1937, a car in which she was a passenger sideswiped a truck, and her arm was nearly severed. Waiting for an ambulance, she lost a lot of blood, and she died in the hospital from shock and internal injuries. She was only forty-three.

Ethel Merman as Annie Oakley in Irving Berlin's musical *Annie Get Your Gun,* in 1946.
(BILLY ROSE THEATRE COLLECTION, THE NEW YORK PUBLIC LIBRARY FOR THE PERFORMING ARTS, ASTOR, LENOX AND TILDEN FOUNDATIONS)

ETHEL MERMAN

La Merm

THE TIME: October 14, 1930. The place: the Alvin Theatre in New York City. It's opening night of a new musical comedy, *Girl Crazy*. The audience, dressed in tuxedos and floor-length gowns, eagerly awaits the new jazzy show by the Gershwin brothers, George and Ira.

There are yelps and cheers as Ethel Merman, a twenty-two-year-old singer who has never played Broadway before, finishes her first song and launches into her second. She's wearing a long black skirt slit almost to the thigh, and a low-cut red blouse. She stands surrounded by thirty chorus girls in skimpy outfits. "I got rhythm, I got music, I got my man—Who could ask for anything more?" Her voice is so strong, it travels out the back of the theater and to the lobby, where it reaches the ears of the ticket takers. When Ethel gets to the end, she sings, "Ah," and holds the C for a thrillingly long eight bars while the orchestra plays the melody underneath. The theater erupts in applause and shouts for encores.

"I Got Rhythm" made Ethel Merman a Broadway star overnight. But it was Ethel herself who kept her star position in musical comedies for an incredible forty years, ending with *Hello, Dolly!* in 1970. Fifteen of her sixteen shows were written expressly for her voice and her stage persona, that of the bold and brassy dame.

Some say Ethel was a "belter." She wasn't. True, she was loud, even without assistance from microphones, since theaters were not miked in the

1930s. But her voice wasn't forced or harsh until later in her life. It was loud as a church bell is loud. Someone called her "a doll from Astoria with a trumpet in her throat," which Ethel loved. She was a straightforward singer who employed only one embellishment. She gave a little flick to her voice when she sang an important word (actually, she added a very short note, on a slightly higher pitch, to the beginning of the word.)

Ethel was proud of her precise pronunciation. It was probably what led Cole Porter, whose lyrics were wordy to the point of tongue-twisting, to say, "I'd rather write songs for Ethel Merman than anyone else in the world."

Ethel never had a musical lesson. Never once did she experience stage fright. She was blessed with a strong diaphragm, she said, which gave her the ability to project a note and hold it. As to breathing, "I just sing until I have to stop and take a breath, then I take it and go on singing."

At least two critics called her singing style "peculiar." Ethel would open her eyes wide, plant her feet firmly onstage, and send her clarion voice to the rafters. In a duet, she rarely looked at the actor to whom she was singing. Instead, she faced the audience, which infuriated the actor but made listeners feel as if they knew her personally.

Unlike most singers who respond to the audience or their own mood, or the musicians in the band, Ethel never varied her performance. "[Watching Ethel] was like watching a train hurtle down the tracks, undeviating, the whole performance radiating zest and spontaneity, and yet you knew that it was exactly the same yesterday, and would be the same the day after," Cole Porter said.

Ethel had an oval face, and eyes that always looked surprised. She was big-busted and had thin, shapely legs. She always wore her brown hair swept up and piled on top of her head, with curls tumbling over her forehead. She wasn't glamour-girl pretty, but that wasn't necessary for a woman in the theater. Being pretty was essential for a movie career in the 1930s, but in the musical theater, a woman had to sing and act. Ethel never had any trouble doing either.

Ethel was born on January 16, 1908, in her parents' bedroom on the third floor of her grandmother's house in Astoria, Queens, in New York City. Ethel's father was a bookkeeper who played piano and taught his daughter how to read music. Every Friday night her parents took Ethel to the Palace

Theatre in Manhattan, New York City, to see a vaudeville show. Sophie Tucker was among Ethel's favorite performers. "When [the vaudevillians would] get out onstage, I'd think, 'Oh, boy, I could do that,'" Ethel said.

So she tried. "I could always sing and I began to entertain when I was

What's New?

FM Radio

Introduced in 1933, FM radio provided better sound with less static than AM radio. Three out of every five homes had a radio, and the American family tuned in for about five hours a day. The cost of the machine aside, radio was free entertainment. People felt comforted knowing they were part of a vast radio audience, whether they were listening to Benny Goodman's dance band, or sidesplitting comedy from George Burns and Gracie Allen, or the Fireside Chats of a popular president, Franklin D. Roosevelt.

Records

The 78 rpm record now held about ten minutes of music on each side. Even on a new record, there were loud snaps, hisses, and pops accompanying the music. After the record was played a hundred or so times, it was completely worn out. Still, records were popular; 85 percent of them were by swing bands, the hot music of the 1930s, and cost fifty cents. Teenagers were big record buyers, especially girls. Girls dressed in short white bobby socks, white buck shoes, pleated skirts, and blouses or close-fitting sweaters, and they danced the jitterbug, the Suzie Q, and the Big Apple.

Most homes still had a windup record player. By 1939, though, a portable model, which plugged in to the radio, could be had for just $9.95.

TV

The most popular exhibit at the 1939 World's Fair in New York City was the pavilion containing twelve television sets. The first TV set was a huge wooden box, about five feet tall, with a tiny, five-inch screen, which showed a black-and-white picture. People stood on long lines to see "radio with pictures," enchanted with the idea of having a little movie theater in their own homes. In 1939, people watched newscasts; a three-act play by Noel Coward called *Hay Fever*; *Vox Pop*, the first audience-participation quiz show; beauty contests; the first telecast baseball game (a college game, Princeton versus Columbia), followed three months later by the first major-league baseball telecast (Brooklyn Dodgers versus Cincinnati Reds)—to name just a few of the offerings on television.

Unfortunately, only the richest people could afford the two-hundred- to six-hundred-dollar TV set. (A brand-new car cost around one thousand dollars.) Just three thousand TVs were sold in 1939.

Broadway (with Times Square in the middle) as Ethel Merman saw it in 1935–36, around the time she was singing in the musical *Anything Goes*. Sophie Tucker was performing in the Loew's State vaudeville theater on the left; her name is on the marquee.
(LIBRARY OF CONGRESS)

five or six," she remembered. Billed as "Little Ethel Zimmermann," she performed at social clubs and charities in and around Astoria. When she was about ten years old, she made American soldiers, who were waiting to be shipped to fight in World War I, cry with a song about her mother: "She's me pal, she's me pal, she's the very best friend that I know."

By the time Ethel was in high school, she knew she wanted to be a singer, but her mother urged her to be more practical, so Ethel took a business course. She quickly found a job as a stenographer and then as a secretary for thirty-five dollars a week. After work, she went home to pick up her suitcase filled with two taffeta dresses and several song sheets, and took the subway into Manhattan to one of several nightclubs, where she sang for seven dollars and fifty cents a night. Deciding Zimmermann was too long a name to put on a marquee, she became Ethel Merman, with her father's consent. The name change inspired the nicknames Mermo, The Merm,

La Merm, and they continue to this day: On the Internet, fans have established a Web site called The Merm Is Perm.

One evening in 1928, an agent heard Ethel and got her a six-month movie contract with Warner Bros. in Hollywood. She quit her secretarial job, made one short film whose title she could never remember later, in which she ran around in a bearskin, and then—the movie company stopped calling. Although the company paid her a generous $125 a week whether she worked or not, she was eager to work and asked to get out of her contract.

She was singing in a vaudeville show in Brooklyn, New York, in 1930 when a hit musical producer came in and liked what he heard. He took Ethel to meet George Gershwin, the most celebrated American composer of the day. Gershwin sat down at his piano, played three songs, and then said, "Miss Merman, if there's anything about these songs you don't like, I'll be most happy to change it." She was so surprised, she said, "No, Mr. Gershwin, they'll do very nicely." The songs were the three that she was to sing in the Broadway musical *Girl Crazy*, including "I Got Rhythm."

Ethel's success was immediate. The poshest nightclub in Manhattan, Casino in the Park, engaged her to sing every night after the curtain closed on *Girl Crazy*. Ethel was making $600 a week in the Broadway show, and another $1,250 at the nightclub—at a time when the average salary, for those who could find work, was $1,300 a *year*.

The Great Depression was on. By 1933, one-quarter of the workforce was unemployed in the United States. People were so poor, they cut strips of rubber from old tires to fill the holes in their shoes. Hungry children knocked on doors on the way to school to ask people for food. In the West, several hundred thousand migrant farmworkers lived in camps without running water. In the North, some men considered themselves lucky to work in a factory for ten cents an hour, and women for four cents.

In 1933 Ethel, on the other hand, was living luxuriously, working in her fourth Broadway hit, *Take a Chance*. Every night she swung her hips in a blood-red satin dress, with a black boa thrown across her shoulders, and sang about a lady named Eadie who "had class with a capital K," to roars of laughter. A thrifty woman, she had saved her money and could afford to move her parents and herself into an elegant new building overlooking

New York's Central Park. Had they arrived the year before, they would have looked out upon "Hoover Valley" (named after President Herbert Hoover), a community of homeless and jobless men who built themselves twenty-nine shacks on the park's Great Lawn. The police eventually ordered the squatters out and destroyed Hoover Valley.

It's hard to understand how Ethel and the theater could do so well while thousands of Americans were actually starving. One reason is that in terrible times people need to escape. Those people who could afford a $3.60 ticket to *Girl Crazy* went to an amusing show that took their minds off such news as someone committing suicide or another business going bankrupt. Of course, $3.60 was a lot when a loaf of bread cost a nickel, so other, cheaper forms of entertainment thrived as well. For just fifteen cents, one could spend all day watching couples struggle to stay on their feet at a dance marathon. For thirty-five cents, one could go to the movies and marvel at the dancing of Fred Astaire and Ginger Rogers, or laugh at the dog Asta, who helped a wealthy gentleman known as "the Thin Man" solve mysteries.

Movies were enormously popular in the thirties, and Ethel, flushed with her theatrical successes, wanted to make movies, too. She went to Hollywood in 1933 and made two films, but they were not particularly successful. Hollywood was a frustrating experience for Ethel, even though she went on to make fourteen movies. She did not appear in the movie versions of most of her musicals, losing out to another actress in all of them except *Anything Goes* and *Call Me Madam*. Ethel didn't fit the mold of a 1930s or 40s movie star; she was not svelte and stunning enough. Her style was too big and brassy, causing directors to say, "Hold it down, Ethel." She felt hampered as she tried to restrain her voice and check her exuberance. She realized her place was in the theater, and to the theater in New York City she returned.

Over the next sixteen years Ethel appeared in eight musicals, all written precisely for her, all but one a hit. From *Anything Goes* in 1934 to *Call Me Madam* in 1950, Ethel worked with the best composers of the day—Cole Porter and Irving Berlin, in particular—who wrote songs to fit her voice and personality. The songs, though usually written for a specific purpose in a specific show, were so timeless and universal that pop and cabaret singers continue to perform and record them today.

The plots of these musicals were silly, and the characters were shallow stereotypes. What made the shows memorable, besides the songs, was Ethel. She had tremendous presence. "No one can match her in putting a song across, in trumpeting its lyrics, in personifying its rhythms," wrote one critic. "She possesses not only great energy, but a kind of shimmering dignity, too; a dignity born of her poise, her skill, her honesty and her magnificent professionalism."

Ethel embodied certain songs so completely that it is impossible not to hear her voice when someone else is singing them: "I Got Rhythm"; "Blow, Gabriel, Blow"; "You're the Top"; "You Can't Get a Man with a Gun"; "Doin' What Comes Natur'lly"; "Everything's Coming Up Roses."

Whether Ethel played a nightclub singer, a movie star, a sharpshooter

Ethel Merman (center) leading the chorus in the song "Blow, Gabriel, Blow" in *Anything Goes,* by Cole Porter, 1935. Ethel played a nightclub singer named Reno Sweeney.
(BILLY ROSE THEATRE COLLECTION, THE NEW YORK PUBLIC LIBRARY FOR THE PERFORMING ARTS, ASTOR, LENOX AND TILDEN FOUNDATIONS)

VANDAMM COLLECTION

or an ambassadress, she was usually the tough-girl type. If she fell in love, she kept the guy at arm's length, singing smart songs like "I Get a Kick Out of You." Or she competed fiercely with him, singing, "Anything you can do, I can do better, I can do anything better than you," as the real-life, pistol-toting Annie Oakley, star of Buffalo Bill's Wild West Show.

In *Annie Get Your Gun* she got to show her softer side when she sang "I Got Lost in His Arms." Her voice is awestruck, almost sweet as she sings, "And I said to my heart as it foolishly kept jumping all around: I got lost, but look what I found." "It was Irving Berlin's lyrics that made a lady out of me," Ethel said gratefully. (Berlin said, "If you write lyrics for Ethel, they

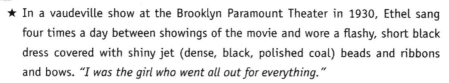

WHAT ETHEL WORE

★ In a vaudeville show at the Brooklyn Paramount Theater in 1930, Ethel sang four times a day between showings of the movie and wore a flashy, short black dress covered with shiny jet (dense, black, polished coal) beads and ribbons and bows. *"I was the girl who went all out for everything."*

★ In *Red, Hot, and Blue!* (1936), Ethel shimmered in a gold dress of paillettes, or long, narrow spangles. On the back was a bustle decorated with a hen sitting in a nest. After the first performance, Ethel strode into her dressing room, fuming. *"The bird goes,"* she said, grabbing a pair of scissors. *"Any audience gets a laugh out of me, gets it while I'm looking at 'em."* She chopped off the hen.

★ In *Call Me Madam* (1950), she wore a silver lamé gown with a long train, which she had to pick up and throw between her legs in order to walk. Ethel told the dressmaker, *"I don't mind a train but you needn't have given me the Super Chief."*

★ Offstage, Ethel wore good jewelry, buying a *"big wad"* of it after every one of her musicals, to remember the show by. For *Panama Hattie* (1940), the first show in which she got top billing, with her name in lights on the theater marquee, she bought a bracelet of two rows of rubies separated by ETHEL A. MERMAN spelled out in diamonds. After all of her jewelry was stolen in a burglary in 1970, Ethel shopped only at flea markets. When she was invited to the White House, she wore a fake diamond brooch she had bought for three dollars.

★ For her everyday dresses, Ethel looked for bargains on Fifth Avenue, for forty or fifty dollars. She favored hemlines at the knee, and pumps with heels to show off her legs to their best advantage. Ethel splurged on evening gowns, which she bought at Wilma's on West 57th Street. Example: a mink-trimmed chartreuse gown for $550.

better be good, for if they're bad everybody's going to hear them.") The musical lasted two years and eight months, the longest run of any of Ethel's shows. Wisely, Ethel had insisted on getting 10 percent of the receipts, which meant she earned a total of $4,700 a week, when the average doctor in America was earning $206 weekly.

Ethel took a businesslike attitude to her work. Later in life, after she sang a concert in London, the audience begged for encores for ten minutes. She thanked them and declined to sing any more. "I haven't any more music rehearsed," she said. Theater critic Kenneth Tynan wrote, "Professional to the gilded hilt, she would not insult her admirers by giving them anything less than perfection."

During rehearsals Ethel noted every word of a director's instructions in shorthand, typed the notes out at home, and returned the next day fully prepared. As much as she demanded of herself, Ethel was also demanding of others. In *Red, Hot, and Blue!* she was supposed to sing the line, "Here I sit above the town in my pet pailletted gown" (a gown covered in paillettes, or flat, long, narrow spangles). She wanted such a dress to sing in. "But a pailletted gown would cost a thousand dollars!" protested the producer. "No gown, no song," Ethel replied. She got the gown.

Ethel's life offstage was as glamorous as the gowns she wore onstage. With Cole Porter and his wife and other celebrities, Ethel moved in a New York social circle known in the press as "café society." Members of this elite set frequented the top clubs, gave fantastic parties, and stayed out till dawn. Ethel had the roomy apartment she shared with her parents, owned lots of furs and expensive jewelry, but she did remain close to her middle-class roots in some ways. She sold her Chrysler touring car and dismissed her chauffeur, saying she found it was easier to walk or take a taxi. She kept the household accounts herself, accurate to the penny. She called herself a meat and potatoes woman and disdained fancy restaurants, but her favorite drink was champagne.

In the 1940s she settled down a little. Her first marriage, to Bill Smith, an actor's agent, was over within days, but a second marriage, to newspaperman Robert Levitt, produced two children, Ethel (whose nickname was Ethel, Jr., although she detested it) and Robert, Jr. (called Bobby). The family moved to a ten-room duplex apartment with a huge terrace, in

Ethel's apartment building. She was as attentive to her children as her grueling schedule of eight shows a week would permit, but her marriage faltered. Ethel said that her husband resented his wife being more famous and earning more than he did. The couple divorced, and in 1953 Ethel married a man named Bob Six, who was the president of Continental Airlines. She moved to Six's hometown of Denver, Colorado, saying that she'd had enough of Broadway and that she wanted to be a mother and a housewife in their newly renovated twenty-eight-room house. Ethel planned to do a little television, some concerts, and maybe a movie or two, but otherwise take it easy and enjoy her freedom. In fact she made one movie, *There's No Business Like Show Business*, and appeared in one television show. By 1956 she was back on Broadway and living in New York City with Six.

Ethel Merman singing with the composer and lyricist Irving Berlin at the time of the musical *Call Me Madam* in 1950. Ethel said his lyrics "made a lady out of me."

The television program, which outclassed anything yet seen on the small screen, was *The Ford Fiftieth Anniversary Show*. In it Ethel and Mary Martin, another big Broadway star, who sang in *Peter Pan* and *The Sound of Music*, sat on high stools and sang a medley of thirty-five songs. The women looked glamorous in tea-length dresses with full skirts, but acted as casual as two girls talking over a backyard fence: "Hi Ethel." "Hi ya, Mary." "How 'bout singing some old songs?" "I think that'd be fun." They traded songs back and forth and sang some duets. They looked relaxed, just like two friends having a great time. In truth, Mary Martin said, they had rehearsed their heads off for twelve hours a day, timing every sound and move to the split second. Their work paid off. In her autobiography, Martin recalled, "I can still hear the applause of the studio audience, see the big laugh in Ethel's eyes." The television program attracted 60 million viewers, more people than Ethel would play to on the stage in her lifetime.

When she was fifty-one years old, Ethel made one last, great debut, as Mama Rose in *Gypsy*. The role was tailor-made for Ethel: a loud, controlling stage mother who pushes her two daughters, June and Rose, into vaudeville. Desperate to give them everything she wished she had herself, Mama Rose acts like a monster and in the end loses both girls. June runs off to get married, and Rose becomes Gypsy Rose Lee, a famous stripper. When the composer Jule Styne played and the lyricist Stephen Sondheim sang the songs for the first time, Ethel burst into tears. "These were dramatic songs with dimension," she said. "[Styne] was reaching out, stretching himself just as I wanted to do."

The show, which she called the "pinnacle" of her career, ended with the brilliant, extended song "Rose's Turn," in which Mama Rose reviews her life. She starts out confidently but breaks down midsong when she

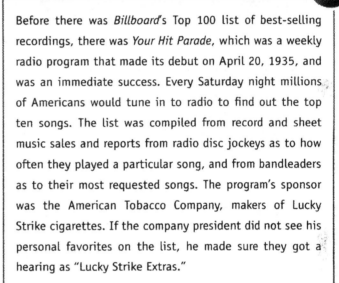

"Your Hit Parade"

Before there was *Billboard*'s Top 100 list of best-selling recordings, there was *Your Hit Parade*, which was a weekly radio program that made its debut on April 20, 1935, and was an immediate success. Every Saturday night millions of Americans would tune in to radio to find out the top ten songs. The list was compiled from record and sheet music sales and reports from radio disc jockeys as to how often they played a particular song, and from bandleaders as to their most requested songs. The program's sponsor was the American Tobacco Company, makers of Lucky Strike cigarettes. If the company president did not see his personal favorites on the list, he made sure they got a hearing as "Lucky Strike Extras."

realizes her daughters are ungrateful for all she has done, that for her it's "Thanks a lot and out with the garbage." Slowly her spirits revive as she understands that it's her turn to thrive: "Everything's coming up roses this time for me, for me, for ME!"

Even the unflappable Ethel Merman found the role of Mama Rose highly demanding. Every night after Act One Ethel sat in her dressing room with her head in her hands, unable to speak. She endured 702 performances, in the middle of which her marriage to Six began to fall apart. After Ethel discovered that he had been unfaithful to her, she divorced him. Then, at the end of an eight-month national *Gypsy* tour, she announced: "I'm through with the theater. From now on I'm living for Ethel."

After *Gypsy*, Ethel lived a quieter life for the next twenty-five years. Her home was a hotel apartment with the kitchen removed, leaving only a refrigerator, since she had never learned to cook. For her meals, she ordered room service. Although Ethel sang some in nightclubs, on television, and even on Broadway, she also did other things. She spent hours on the phone and loved gossip. She collected Raggedy Ann and Andy dolls and did needlepoint with a passion.

Ethel on Broadway: Her Sixteen Musicals

Girl Crazy, 1930

George White's Scandals, 1931

Humpty Dumpty, 1932 (closed during tryouts)

Take a Chance, 1932

Anything Goes, 1934

Red, Hot, and Blue!, 1936

Stars in Your Eyes, 1939

Du Barry Was a Lady, 1939

Panama Hattie, 1940

Something for the Boys, 1943

Annie Get Your Gun, 1946

Call Me Madam, 1950

Happy Hunting, 1956

Gypsy, 1959

Annie Get Your Gun (revival), 1966

Hello, Dolly!, 1970

In 1964 Ethel had a brief fourth marriage, to actor Ernest Borgnine, which broke up during the honeymoon. To lift her spirits, Ethel took a world tour with her son, Bobby, who was nineteen, traveling to Japan, Hong Kong, Thailand, India, Russia, and Finland. Ethel's daughter, Ethel Geary, meanwhile, had married and had two children, but suffered from depression. In 1967, six months after young Ethel's husband had obtained a divorce and custody of their children, Ethel Geary died at the age of twenty-five from an overdose of pills. The death was possibly a suicide, but Ethel Merman always denied it.

Ethel appeared on Broadway for the last time in *Hello, Dolly!* at age sixty-two. "There she still is, cocky, chin tilted, half-dollar eyes sprouting sunburst black lashes, power flowing from her that will still light the town when Con Edison fails," wrote drama critic Walter Kerr in the *New York Times.*

On February 15, 1984, Ethel died of a brain tumor at the age of seventy-six. Five days later, a long black limousine drove slowly down Broadway. Inside, Bobby held the urn containing his mother's ashes. At 7:59 P.M., one minute before eight o'clock, curtain time, the lights on all the theater marquees on Broadway dimmed in a final, respectful remembrance of La Merm.

Ethel Merman typing in the late 1950s. She always handled her own accounts and correspondence: "I wouldn't hire a secretary because I can do better myself." As a teenager she took a four-year business course and then worked as a secretary before performing in her first Broadway show.
(LIBRARY OF CONGRESS)

Movie stars of
the 1940s were
expected to be
glamorous: Judy
Garland posing
for a fashion
shoot for
*Photoplay-Movie
Mirror* magazine
in 1942.

JUDY GARLAND

The Girl Next Door

THE CAST of teenagers was assembled in costume, on a trolley. The crew was ready to shoot the scene. But one actress was missing, the figure around whom the whole scene would revolve. Twenty-one-year-old Judy Garland was in her dressing room, refusing to come out.

Actress Mary Astor, who was playing Judy's mother, knocked on Judy's door. "Judy, what's happened to you? You were a trouper—once," she said.

Judy didn't reply.

"You have kept the entire company out there waiting for two hours," Mary continued. "Waiting for you to favor us with your presence. You know we're stuck—there's nothing we can do without you."

Judy giggled and said she had heard that from others in the cast.

"Well, then, either get the hell on set or I'm going home," Miss Astor shouted.

Eventually Judy did emerge, and played one of her best scenes, in the movie *Meet Me in St. Louis* (1944). Judy's riding the trolley with her friends when the boy she is crazy about hops aboard, which causes her to burst into song: "Zing, zing, zing went my heart strings." Her bright voice sounds at once breathless and secure. Her brown button eyes are shining and she glides through the trolley car. Anyone watching can't take his or her eyes off of her.

Judy Garland was one of the most difficult movie stars in Hollywood. She suffered from physical and emotional problems, which constantly delayed production, added to movies' costs, and generally drove coworkers,

Judy Garland was fifteen and Sophie Tucker was fifty when they made a movie together called _Broadway Melody of 1938_. Sophie played Judy's mother.

particularly producers and directors, crazy with frustration. But when Judy worked, she _worked_, throwing every inch of her five-foot frame into the scene at hand. There was no sign, in any of her thirty-six movies, of the trouble it took for her to make them.

She was a phenomenally quick study. "Judy looked at a script once—and never flubbed a line," said Joe Pasternak, who produced four of her movies. "She learned a musical number in no time and she gave it her all. Very seldom did you have to make two takes with her. This was very unusual—a normal musical comedy star would take three or four weeks to learn a number."

Dancer-actor Gene Kelly, who starred with Judy in the movie _The Pirate_, called Judy "the finest all-round performer we ever had in America." She could not only sing, but she could act, dance, and make people laugh.

Judy Garland was born Frances Gumm on June 10, 1922, to a pair of former vaudevillians who owned a movie theater in the small town of Grand Rapids, Minnesota. Vaudeville was nearing its end, soon to be replaced by the movies, but people still enjoyed vaudeville as "An Extra Added Attraction" at the picture show. One evening the Gumms hired three little girls called the Blue Sisters to perform at intermission, and Frances sat entranced, bouncing up and down, humming along. When the performance was over, she asked, "Can I do that, Daddy?"

A few months later Frances joined her two older sisters at their parents' theater, singing "When My Sugar Walks Down the Street" and doing a tap dance. At the end she sang "Jingle Bells" by herself, over and over, as the audience asked for more. She was two years old.

"The roar of the crowd—that wonderful, wonderful sound—is something I've been breathing in since I was two years old," Judy said years later, after she had become addicted to several kinds of medication. "It's like taking nineteen hundred wake-up pills."

When the Gumm Sisters became an act, it was little Frances who attracted the most notice. "All do so well in their specialties that the discrimination of special mention is hardly just, but the remarkable work of Baby Frances particularly appeals to hearers because of her diminutive size and few years," wrote a reviewer in Los Angeles. Frances was seven years old.

Judy Garland at twenty-one, standing on the trolley in the movie *Meet Me in St. Louis.*

At twelve, she was "a roly poly girl with eyes like saucers," according to one observer. She also had a new name. "Judy" came from a popular song with a lyric Frances liked: "If you think she's a saint and you find out she ain't, that's Judy." "Garland" came about when an actor who thought "Gumm" unflattering introduced the Gumm sisters as "the Garland Sisters," in Chicago.

Meanwhile, in Hollywood, movie studios were signing up lots of child actors for the happy-go-lucky family pictures that the public wanted to see. Judy got an audition at Metro-Goldwyn-Mayer (MGM), one of the so-called "Big Five" studios, in Culver City, California. "She sang 'Zing, Went the Strings of My Heart,' and I almost fell off the piano bench," said Roger Edens, who accompanied Judy on the piano. "[She] couldn't read music, but [she] didn't have to. Her talent was inborn."

Judy signed her first MGM contract when she was thirteen years old, for one hundred dollars a week for seven years. Astoundingly, considering her later success and MGM's many renewals of that contract, the studio didn't know what to do

Television

A ten-inch television set cost about $375, when the average yearly salary was $2,600, so by 1947, only 250,000 sets had been sold. If you were the first on your block to have television, you could expect the neighbors on your doorstep, eager to see anything "on the box," even the TV test patterns.

What else did they see?

Everything, including: puppets; news; serious plays; a game show with five-dollar cash prizes; magic acts; a house-wife cooking; a man showing his coin collection; and lots and lots of comedy—some of it unintentional. All of TV was live, and accidents were a daily occurrence. A Western once got interrupted by a horrendous noise: a horse chewing on a microphone "hidden" in a hitching post. In the studio, lights were so hot that singer Hildegarde's mascara ran down her cheeks. A man hastily crawled under the table beside her and held out a handkerchief—on camera, of course. Hildegarde pretended the whole thing was part of the act, mopped her face, and went on singing.

with Judy at first. It took two years for them to cast her in a full-length feature film, and then it was because of a song. She had been begging Mr. Edens, now her musical director, to let her sing "Drums in My Heart," a favorite song of Ethel Merman's. He said she was too young, but Judy pestered him until he said, "Go to lunch, Judy. If I haven't written something you like better by the time you get back—you win!"

When Judy returned, Edens played "Dear Mr. Gable," about a girl writing a fan letter to the actor Clark Gable. Judy learned the song in an hour and sang it to Mr. Gable as a birthday present. She got a hug from the glamorous actor, and sang the song in her first full-length MGM film, *Broadway Melody of 1938*, which also featured Sophie Tucker. Next, MGM put her in several comedies with children in them, all starring Mickey Rooney. Typically, Judy played a plain sort of girl who hankered after Rooney, while he, in turn, favored other, prettier girls. Only in *Andy Hardy Meets Debutante* did her character finally win his affection, and all she got was a kiss on the cheek. She was still wearing little-girl dresses with puffed sleeves and a lace collar, although she was eighteen years old and sounded far from girlish when she delivered "I'm Nobody's Baby." She sang in a shimmering, silvery voice, with clear diction and complete authority.

If MGM was deaf and blind to Judy's womanliness, it was because she was making piles of money for them as a child, and in the movie business, the theory was that if a formula worked, why change it? Years later, after she had left MGM, Judy remained angry about the studio's reluctance to let her grow up. "Anywhere else in the world, once you're out of high school, have celebrated your nineteenth birthday, and drive a car, you automatically step out of the Junior Miss class. But in Hollywood people won't forget how you looked when you were 'that age.'" For Judy, "that" age was about fifteen.

America was fighting in World War II from 1941 to 1945, and Judy's youthfulness, cheerful innocence, and songbirdlike voice had immense appeal as a kind of escape valve. After the war, Americans mourning both their personal losses and the horrors committed in Europe and Asia responded to something else in Judy's voice, a feeling of vulnerability that is rare in a popular singer. Listening to her, perhaps people found the courage to open their own hearts to conflicting, painful feelings of hope and despair, anticipation and disappointment.

Hollywood was in its heyday in the 1940s, and Judy made an average of two movies a year in the decade, every one of them a success. More people were going to the movies than ever before: 90 million a week. A movie ticket cost thirty-four cents, and 70 percent of the movies came from just five studios. The movie studio system was known as "the factory" because its goal was to make movies quickly and efficiently in order to turn a big profit, and because the studios exerted control over every aspect of filmmaking. They not only produced the movies but distributed them and owned the theaters in which the movies were shown. They gave actors five- or seven-year contracts and expected them to make as many movies as needed.

A major star like Judy often worked on more than one picture at a time. She was also expected to keep her name in the spotlight by making musical recordings and public appearances. From 1940 to 1945 Judy recorded thirty-five sides for Decca (a record had one song per side); sang on more than seventy-five radio programs; and performed in hundreds of stage shows to entertain World War II troops or to raise money for the war effort. In these stage shows, too, she worked

What's New?

LP—The Long-playing Record

In 1948, the Columbia Company introduced the long-playing record, or LP, a twelve-inch disc made of vinyl that played at 33⅓ revolutions per minute (rpm) and enabled a listener to hear a whole symphony. RCA, whose interests ran in the more popular vein, countered with a small, vinyl 45 rpm disc, containing a single song per side, and an accompanying turntable that sold for just $12.95. The "battle of the speeds" was on. Consumers had a choice between 33⅓ LPs, 45s, or the old shellac 78s.

In the movie *The Wizard of Oz,* Judy Garland played Dorothy, a girl who was lost in Oz and trying to find her way home to Kansas. Here she appears in the crystal ball of the Wicked Witch of the West.

(EMMA DRYDEN COLLECTION)

harder than most, doing five shows a day, sometimes in two different states, and giving the boys a dozen songs per show instead of the usual five or six. To the soldiers, Judy was "the girl next door." She was not a glamour queen, but was natural and friendly and wholesome, just like the women the boys had left back home.

For all her work Judy was well rewarded by MGM. Her weekly salary was $2,000 at a time when a bottle of soda cost a nickel, a magazine cost a quarter, and a factory worker could support a family of four on $40 a week. Judy's wages increased dramatically over the course of the decade, to $2,500, then $3,000, and finally, $5,600 a week in 1946. MGM also gave her a red Cadillac, her first car, when she was seventeen, and threw a big party for her at the studio president's mansion when she turned eighteen.

Judy paid a high price for her rewards. In 1941, she eloped with band leader David Rose and got married in Las Vegas. MGM found out and told her to forget about a honeymoon and to report back to work within twenty-four hours. When the studio wanted her to lose some weight, she was kept on a strict diet of chicken broth and cottage cheese. She was hungry all the time. If she snitched a malted milk shake, spies reported it to the studio president.

The most serious aspect of MGM's control over actors was its practice of dispensing drugs. Diet pills came first. As Judy explained later, "[Dispensing diet pills] was to the studio's financial advantage to keep their investment neat and photogenic and, to some extent, happy. But my primary function was to work. As long as I worked, the studio's investment in the property known as Garland paid off. If I got fat, I couldn't work. So, I mustn't get fat."

The diet pills contained amphetamines, which made Judy peppy and unable to sleep at night. So she was given sleeping pills, which caused her to be groggy at seven in the morning, when she was expected in the makeup department. So Judy was given another pill to wake up. Prescribing medication to increase an actor's performance was not at all unusual in the studio system. The problem was, Judy was only fifteen years old when she began taking pills, and she became addicted to them.

"They are giving me pills of some kind to go to sleep, and then others to give me energy when I'm awake. And I don't feel good on those pills," Judy complained during the making of *Meet Me in St. Louis* in 1943. Although she tried several times during her life to kick the drug habit, she was unsuccessful. Instead she became increasingly proficient in procuring pills against her doctor's orders and figured out ways to hide pills, even sewing them into the hems of her clothes.

After the war ended, MGM apparently thought Americans were ready to see Judy grow up, and gave Judy her first grown-up part in a movie musical, *The Harvey Girls*, in 1946. Judy was twenty-four and played a mail-order bride of approximately the same age, who discovers her groom is not what he said he was, and becomes a waitress instead. The story was based on those of real young women who traveled by train to the Western frontier in the 1890s to work as waitresses in a chain of restaurants owned by Fred Harvey. Judy was a bona fide star by this time, with enough clout to choose her own costume designer. As she gets off the train she looks radiant. She wears a long, sky-blue dress with a close-fitting bodice and full circle skirt, which makes her waist look tiny, an extravagant blue hat with white flowers and yellow netting, and white gloves. The townspeople have gathered to greet the passengers, and everybody sings "On the Atchison, Topeka and the Santa Fe," an infectious tune with clickety-clack rhythms and romantic lyrics.

To prepare for the scene, all Judy did was watch a stand-in do one run-through. Then she said, "I'm ready," and she performed the scene perfectly, with every movement of the stand-in memorized and every motion matched to the subtle changes in her voice.

As professional as she was in those moments, Judy missed eleven days of shooting and was late on nearly forty occasions during the five months of filming *The Harvey Girls.* She explained why: "I was a nervous wreck, jumpy and irritable from sleeping too little. I couldn't take the tension at the studio. Everything at MGM was competition. Every day I went to work with tears in my eyes. Work gave me no pleasure. The studio had become a haunted house for me. It was all I could do to keep from screaming every time the director looked at me."

Despite a high level of inner turmoil, Judy managed to build and sustain a thirty-year career, first in movies, then on the concert stage. The question that has baffled her biographers is: How did she do it? Perhaps Judy's talent was simply so large that it overpowered her difficulties. An example of the immensity of her gift comes in *The Wizard of Oz* (1939), her best-known picture, when she sings "Over the Rainbow." Judy's character, Dorothy, seems to be a girl of about twelve, dressed in a pinafore and anklet socks, her hair in pigtails. (In fact, Judy was seventeen years old, and had to have her breasts bound and flattened against her chest to make her look younger for the movies.) But Dorothy *sounds* like a woman, an experienced singer with clear diction and a precise, sure way of phrasing the melody. In the movie Judy sang with a directness that seemed to rip through the movie screen and bring her right into the theater. Beneath the sunny exterior of her voice was a sense of the hurts and troubles she had experienced. Even as a teenager she had a vulnerability that touched all who listened carefully to her singing.

Judy's personal life was almost as turbulent as her professional life. She married five times and went through four divorces. After divorcing David

Rose, she married the movie director Vincent Minnelli in 1945. Judy married again, in 1952, to Sid Luft, who became her manager. The two marriages produced three children who were very dear to Judy: two daughters who became singers and actresses, Liza Minnelli and Lorna Luft, and a son, Joey Luft.

Meanwhile, in 1950, when Judy was twenty-eight, MGM decided it had had enough of its temperamental star, and suspended her. Publicly, Judy

 HAT JUDY WORE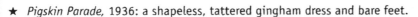

Judy's Movie Wardrobe:

★ *Pigskin Parade,* 1936: a shapeless, tattered gingham dress and bare feet.

★ *The Wizard of Oz,* 1939: a snug-fitting gingham pinafore, white blouse with puffed sleeves, white anklets, and red patent-leather shoes.

★ *The Pirate,* 1946: a white satin wedding dress costing $3,313, trimmed with handmade antique lace from France and embroidered with a thousand pearls; five petticoats.

★ *Easter Parade,* 1946: oversized man's suit, patched and ragged; bow tie; top hat; floppy, clownish shoes (she and Fred Astaire played tramps and sang "A Couple of Swells").
Note: The makeup supervisor on *Meet Me in St. Louis* threw out the rubber disks that had been inserted in Judy's nose to change its shape, and the caps on her teeth. "You don't need all this junk. You're a pretty girl," she said. Nevertheless, she did use makeup to raise Judy's eyebrows and give her a fuller lower lip, and she altered Judy's hairline with tweezers.

Judy in Concert:

★ London, 1951: a lemon-colored dress with a flared organdy skirt, and diamond earrings, necklace, bracelet, and belt buckle—"an ensemble that cheerfully upholds her reputation as the worst-dressed woman on the screen," wrote a critic for the *Daily Express.*

★ New York, 1956: a black taffeta dress with numerous skirts, one of which became dislodged. *"Something always happens to me,"* Judy said, and disappeared backstage for repairs.

On TV:

★ *The Judy Garland Show,* 1963: chic sheaths that showed off Judy's slim legs.

For a Photo Shoot:

★ Group photo of MGM stars, *Life* magazine, 1949: a black blouse and pale skirt. Actress Katherine Hepburn, dressed in slacks, commented to Judy, *"I knew I'd be badly dressed, and I knew you'd be badly dressed. The only difference is that you took the time."*

Judy Garland, age thirty-two, looking out the window of a train.
(MUSEUM OF MODERN ART FILM STILLS ARCHIVE)

took the close of her MGM career in stride. "I was a very tired girl, and now maybe Metro realizes that. They were terribly nice about letting me out of my contract—it was fine of them and good for me. I feel like I've shed a suit of armor."

There was probably some truth in what she said, but Judy was not happy. She locked herself in the bathroom at home and tried to kill herself by cutting her throat with a broken water glass. The wound was slight, but the feelings behind it were not: "I felt humiliated and unwanted—and faced with the bitter knowledge that I'd come to that unhappy position by my own actions."

Judy need not have blamed herself entirely. Hollywood's heyday was coming to an end. Weekly attendance at the movies declined by one half between 1947 and 1957, for several reasons. After World War II ended in 1945, soldiers came home and went to college, cutting down on their leisure—moviegoing—time. They also married and had children, which kept adults at home and tuned to the radio instead of out at the movies. Finally, television was about to overtake both movies and radio as the next great entertainment, expanding from ten thousand television sets sold in 1946 to four million sets sold in 1950. TV, though still in black and white, was free, once you owned a set.

As it turned out, Judy didn't need the movies. In 1951, she got herself booked into the Palace, a former vaudeville theater in New York City.

There were doubts that the public would turn out for vaudeville, even with Judy Garland as the star attraction and at the relatively low price of $4.80 for a good seat, but on opening night, five thousand fans were waiting *outside* the theater, hoping for a glimpse of the star. Inside, Judy sang "Shine on Harvest Moon" and Sophie Tucker's signature tune, "Some of These Days," as well as songs from her movies: "You Made Me Love You," "The Boy Next Door," and "The Trolley Song," and "seemed to be neither male nor female, young nor old, pretty nor plain," wrote critic Clifton Fadiman. "She had no 'glamor,' only magic." At the end of the concert, when "she breathed the last phrases of 'Over the Rainbow' and cried out its universal, unanswerable query, 'why can't I?,' it was as though the bewildered hearts of all the people in the world had moved quietly together and become one, shaking in Judy's throat, and there breaking." Almost everyone in the audience was crying, *Life* magazine reported.

The Palace show ran for nineteen weeks, dispelling any doubts about Judy's fame and future. "With such encouragement I can do anything," she said.

Judy went on to have a second career as a stage singer, but she also made six more movies for other studios, including *A Star Is Born* in 1954. The movie included the enthralling eighteen-minute musical sequence, "Born in a Trunk," which traced the rise of a vaudevillian, recalling Judy's early years. "Judy Garland makes a stunning comeback," wrote a critic in *Time* magazine. Judy also appeared frequently on television and even hosted her own program, *The Judy Garland Show*, in 1963.

To her fans, Judy was always more than a singer, actress, and entertainer. She was someone with whom they could identify. Her followers tracked faithfully her well-publicized marriages and divorces (she married briefly twice more, to Mark Herron, an actor, and to Mickey Deans, a disco manager), her hospitalizations, sellouts, and no-shows. In her last decade, ill, exhausted, performing with only a shred of a voice left but still a stunning presence, Judy became something else again: a survivor. When she died at age forty-seven—"an accidental death by an incautious dose of barbituates," said the coroner—on June 22, 1969, twenty-two thousand of her fans came to view the body at the funeral home, which stayed open all night to accommodate the crowd.

Anita O'Day,
famous for
wearing mannish
clothes, donned
a gown for a
television
appearance
in 1958.

ANITA O'DAY

Jazz Gypsy

TO ANITA O'DAY, the Newport Jazz Festival of 1958 was just a "swinging gig." The festival in Newport, Rhode Island, was the only such event that counted among jazz fans and musicians, and it was nice for Anita to be in company with such greats as trumpet player Louis Armstrong and pianist Duke Ellington. Dressed in a slim, black sheath and a large, black, wide-brimmed hat trimmed in white feathers, Anita looked chic as she climbed the steps to the outdoor stage.

Anita had no idea she was being filmed—her drummer, John Poole, had signed her name to a release form giving permission to a film crew. When the movie, a documentary about the festival called *Jazz on a Summer's Day*, came out a year later, it took Anita by surprise, and suddenly everyone was talking about Anita O'Day and her two numbers, "Sweet Georgia Brown" and "Tea for Two." She hadn't sung them straight but had twisted the melody and chopped up the rhythm so the songs sounded completely fresh.

Newsweek raved about her, and the *New York Times* ran a glowing review that said: "Anita O'Day making mincemeat of 'Sweet Georgia Brown' and 'Tea for Two' is as vivid and insinuating as is Mahalia Jackson [also on the program] booming 'The Lord's Prayer.'" *Jazz on a Summer's Day* became a jazz-cult favorite and a turning point in Anita's career. It gave everyone who had been buying Anita's albums a rare chance, in pre-videotape days, to put an image of the singer with the sound of the singer. "I've thought about it a lot," Anita said, "and I've concluded that the fact I looked so together after all the horrendous things [people had] read about me going through caught their imaginations."

The "horrendous things" Anita referred to were several arrests and two jail terms for drug possession. Anita was a heroin addict. She was, in fact, "high as a kite" (her words) on that particular summer's day in 1958. That she was able to do good work, even some of her best work, while hooked on an addictive drug is one of the mysteries of Anita's own story and her whole era. Many, many jazz musicians were addicted to heroin in the 1940s and 50s. Saxophone player Charlie Parker died at the age of thirty-four, and singer Billie Holiday died at forty-four, from ailments related to drug and alcohol addiction. It's possible they would have been greater artists without drugs, but of course we'll never know. Anita was lucky. After an overdose and near-death, she did manage to kick the habit in 1968, when she was forty-eight years old.

Anita doesn't have a pretty voice. She has a husky sound and an imprecise sense of pitch. Fortunately, in jazz, it's not what a singer has but what she does with it, how she manipulates the notes and how she plays with and against the others in the band. Unlike pop singers, who deliver a song more or less as written, jazz singers alter freely the tune, rhythm, and/or words, or even abandon the words altogether for nonsense syllables like "she bob da boo," which is called scat singing. As Anita herself explained it: "I want to make music. That is, to use my voice as an instrument."

Anita was a free spirit in music and in life. Once, when she was auditioning for Benny Goodman, the country's top bandleader, he complained that she wasn't singing the melody.

"I don't sing the melody on songs like this one. Everybody already knows the melody," she replied.

"In my band, the girl singer sings the melody," countered Goodman.

Anita walked out of the room. "He wanted me to sing the melody and I don't always feel that," she said simply.

Anita Belle Colton was born on October 18, 1919, in Chicago, Illinois. She grew up poor. Her father abandoned her family when Anita was a baby, and her mother went to work in a box factory. Mother and daughter were not close, but they had one thing in common: the radio. It was turned on day and night in their one-room-and-kitchenette apartment, and they listened devotedly to the musical programs. From the age of two, Anita spent the summers with her grandparents in Kansas City, where she was introduced to church and singing hymns. When she was in kindergarten, she got the leading part singing and dancing in the Christmas play. "It was one of the few times Mom showed any pride in me when I was a kid," Anita said. Otherwise school was a painful experience for Anita, because she had trouble learning to read, probably because she needed glasses. "In my mind, I wasn't worth a whole lot and nobody went out of the way to make me feel good about myself," she remembered.

When Anita was fourteen years old, she left home, with her mother's consent, to be a professional walkathon contestant. Walkathons and dance marathons were a popular form of entertainment in which couples walked,

Anita O'Day at the 1958 Newport Jazz Festival, where her renditions of "Sweet Georgia Brown" and "Tea for Two" earned glowing reviews.
(MUSIC DIVISION, THE NEW YORK PUBLIC LIBRARY FOR THE PERFORMING ARTS, ASTOR, LENOX AND TILDEN FOUNDATIONS)

or danced, for hours and days on end (except for periodic fifteen-minute breaks), for money, while an audience cheered them on. Anita took the name O'Day: "In pig Latin it meant 'dough,' which was what I hoped to make." She was not disappointed. In her first walkathon, in Muskegon, Michigan, she lasted 782 hours, 216 of which were spent chained to her partner, and earned ninety-five dollars. Not bad for 1933, when a good breakfast of eggs, bacon, and toast cost fifteen cents.

Money wasn't the only reason Anita enjoyed the marathons. As an added attraction, contestants were encouraged to display their talents, so Anita got to sing. Viewers threw coins if they liked the performance, and Anita said, "I can still remember the shiver that went up my spine as two big silver dollars clattered to the floor after I sang 'Is It True What They Say About Dixie?'"

Anita spent two years in the grueling endurance business, and quit only when a truant officer caught up to her and sent her back to school in Chicago.

But school held no interest for Anita. "Senn Junior High had my body between 9:00 A.M. and 4:00 P.M., but my mind was wandering the taverns of the Uptown district," she said. She got a job dancing in a chorus line in a tavern when she was about sixteen years old. One night, filling in for the solo singer, who was out sick, she performed "I Can't Give You Anything But Love, Baby." Anita got the singer's job.

Improvisation: "A Bagful of Polka Dots"

Improvisation is the heart of jazz. It's also what separates jazz from most other kinds of popular music. Jazz musicians feel free to change the melody, harmony, rhythm, and even words to make the music their own. And they generally do it on the spot. In her autobiography, *High Times, Hard Times,* Anita O'Day offered a window into the mind of a jazz improviser. One night at the Off-Beat Club in Chicago, when she was nineteen, she was faced with more time onstage than she had songs. She decided to stretch out her last number, "Oh, Lady, Be Good," by adding improvised choruses, twelve in all. Here's what she was thinking as she sang: "I needed an idea from somewhere. I saw a polka dot blouse [in the audience]. So I developed that chorus as a bagful of polka dots. . . . I looked around the room and that gave me the idea of singing the structure of the room—long wall, short wall, long wall, short wall. That gave me the frame for that chorus. I turned to the band. Five men. So I put [the song] into a five rhythm. Anything that I could get an idea from, I put to work to fill out my time on the stand."

Anita apparently did far more than fill time. When she finished after twelve choruses, "people shouted, stamped, applauded, whistled, stood on their chairs and cheered."

Meanwhile, her approach to getting a musical education was decidedly low-key. "I took whatever I could use from wherever I could find it," she said. An older man, Al Lyons, who was a comic and a guitar player, took her aside and played recordings by singers, telling her what to listen for in Mildred Bailey, Ella Fitzgerald, Billie Holiday, and others. Her first boyfriend seduced her to the accompaniment of Louis Armstrong records. Anita listened closely to Armstrong's singing. "His timing was impeccable. He phrased in unexpected ways. Most interesting to me was that he had no tone at all."

Anita, too, had very little tone, which is to say she was unable to sustain a note for very long or give it a full sound. She had no vibrato—the intentional vocal wobble that the best singers use discriminately to enhance a note or a phrase. Try as she might, she'd never sound even remotely like her fellow jazz singer Sarah Vaughan, known for the sheer sonic beauty of her tone as well as extraordinary range and power. Anita thought later that her own singing problems came from having no uvula (the cylindrical mass of tissue that hangs at the back of one's mouth); a surgeon had accidentally sliced it off during a tonsillectomy when she was seven years old. One way that she got around her difficulty was to deliver a song in rapid-fire eighth and sixteenth notes instead of the usual, slower quarter notes. Being rhythmically inventive came naturally, but Anita's gift was further developed during a brief, unconsummated marriage to a drummer, Don Carter, when she was seventeen. Carter gave her drum lessons on his drum practice pad and filled their Chicago apartment with drummers and other musicians. Anita was in heaven. "Man, I was living and learning."

Anita sang in every Chicago tavern she could: The Planet Mars, Ball of Fire (where she was billed as "The Princess of Swing"), and Vialago, which had a glass dance floor. She began to think she had "a real shot" at being a singer. "When I went on stage and sang 'It's De-Lovely' or 'Organ Grinder's Swing,' I got the love I craved. I didn't need anyone. For me, music equalled love." While she was working, at age nineteen, as a singing waitress for $22.50 a week, an editor at *Down Beat*, the leading trade newspaper for musicians, stopped in and heard her. He was opening a new club with a partner; would she like to sing three sets between 10:00 P.M. and

4:00 A.M. for $125 a week? "A hundred and twenty-five and I don't waitress? Where?" Anita jumped at the chance.

Down Beat announced the opening of the Off-Beat Club in a headline loaded with jazz lingo: HEP CATS TO GET NEW DEAL WITH MINIATURE SWING CONCERTS, NEW TALENT, RIBS AND JIVE ON TAP. Opening night, Anita had to go on with no rehearsal, since decorators had been working onstage right up until showtime. She had twenty-four minutes to fill and only five songs in her repertoire. When Anita got to her last number, "Oh, Lady, Be Good," she improvised chorus after chorus to fill time. At the end the audience exploded. "It was the response you dream about, made sweeter by the fact that it came from people who understood what I was doing."

Two years later, in 1939, the great, flamboyant drummer Gene Krupa asked Anita to join his band, which was considered one of the best in the country. All the so-called "big bands" had a vocalist, almost always a woman, who was referred to variously as the "canary," "chirper," or "girl singer." Anita was thrilled to get the job, but she balked at the "uniform" she was told to wear—a full-length gown. Anita told Krupa she couldn't afford the gowns on a salary of forty dollars a week (room and board included), and, anyway, it was impossible to keep them clean and pressed while traveling every night on a bus. "I'm not your ordinary peaches and cream band chick," she said. "I want them to listen to me, not look at me. I want to be treated like another musician." She proposed an alternative to Krupa: a jacket, like the men in the band wore, and a skirt and white shirt. She

Gene Krupa, drummer and bandleader. Anita O'Day helped put his band on the map when she was hired as its featured singer, or canary.
(MUSIC DIVISION, THE NEW YORK PUBLIC LIBRARY FOR THE PERFORMING ARTS, ASTOR, LENOX AND TILDEN FOUNDATIONS)

promised that when the band played ballrooms, she would wear a gown. Krupa agreed.

The new outfit suited her style, which was different from that of the other canaries. "Anita came across strictly as a hip jazz musician. She would dress in a suit similar to those of the musicians, and when she'd sing she'd come on strong, full of fire, with an either-you-like-me-or-you-don't-but-if-you-don't-it's-your-loss attitude," said big-band historian George Simon.

Down Beat named Anita the new star of the year in 1941, the same year she gave Krupa the biggest hit he ever had, "Let Me Off Uptown." The song was a light little thing, a swinging mixture of dialogue, song, and trumpet solo by Roy Eldridge. To start, Anita asked Roy if he'd been uptown. "What's uptown?" answered Roy. Anita sang the answer: "They got rib joints, juke joints, hep joints, where could a fella go to top it?" She was relaxed and cool and singing a little flat, in a lazy, seemingly on-purpose kind of way. Then Eldridge entered in complete contrast, searing the ears with a high-pitched horn solo.

For Anita and other girl singers, the big band offered a musical education that couldn't be had anywhere else. Peggy Lee, one of the best singers of the 1950s, said: "I learned more about music from the men I worked with in bands than I've learned anywhere else. They taught me discipline and the value of rehearsing and how to train."

When the big bands began dissolving after World War II ended in 1945, some singers, like Peggy Lee, were able to make the transition from canary to solo artist. It took Anita almost ten years to make that move, and in the interim she did little singing. For one thing, she had begun to use drugs, first marijuana, then heroin, and she got arrested three times for drug possession and served two jail terms. For another, jazz was changing—both the music and its place in the American culture. Instead of being *the* popular music, heard all over the radio and in every big club and dance hall, jazz became almost obscure. It moved into small clubs and evolved into "bebop," a more dissonant and complex style than swing. The new music acquired a certain status: jazz became "hip" and "cool" among intellectuals—people who liked to study and discuss philosophy, sociology, literature, and political science—and rebellious types involved

What's New?

Pop Music on TV

Your Hit Parade went from radio to television in 1950, because, for the first time, more Americans were watching TV than listening to the radio. The most popular feature of the show was Ten Top Tunes of the Week, which might have included a novelty song like Rosemary Clooney's "Come On-a My House," or a romantic ballad like "I'll See You in My Dreams" by Doris Day. The yardstick for selecting Top Tunes was never disclosed, although reference was made to sale of sheet music, jukebox plays, record sales, and performances on radio and television. The show ended in 1959, killed in part by rock and roll and by *American Bandstand*.

American Bandstand went on the air as a live, national TV show on August 5, 1957. The host, Dick Clark, played rock-and-roll records while teenagers danced the latest dances, like the Bunny Hop and the Stroll. By that time, jazz was out of the mainstream and no longer considered dance music, so 20 million kids rushed home from school to watch *American Bandstand* each afternoon from 2:30 to 5:30. The teenagers who appeared onscreen had to be at least fourteen and follow a strict dress code: jackets for the boys, and skirts for girls; and no jeans, tight-fitting sweaters, or T-shirts. Occasionally performers like Connie Francis ("Where the Boys Are") and Jerry Lee Lewis ("Great Balls of Fire") made live appearances, but they always lip-synched, or mimed the words, to records. The show ran for thirty-two years.

in radical politics. The lingo made its way into the 1954 hit movie *The Wild One*, in which actor Marlon Brando's hoodlum buddies heckle an old man: "Did you pick up on this jive, man? Did you dig the rebop? Give me some skin."

Thanks to a piece of good luck, O'Day finally went solo in 1955. Producer Norman Granz was starting up a record label, Verve, and he had hired an arranger named Buddy Bregman. When Bregman saw Anita's name on the list of possible singers, he remembered that they had both gone to the same junior high school back in Chicago. "I'll take a chance on O'Day," he said.

Everything about their first recording session was right, from the material Bregman chose—twelve "groovy songs that ordinary people as well as jazz buffs liked," said Anita—to the location—an old theater with great acoustics—to the band—"Class A studio musicians who ate well and slept in the same bed every night, cats who could really get the music going," Anita said. "The sound engineer was also tops . . . he made sure to keep my voice on top." This was important, because unlike in later years, when the various instruments and the vocals were recorded on separate tracks and "mixed" into one recording afterward, in 1955 an engineer had to get the correct balance between the voice and the band during the recording session.

The album, *Anita*, was a success. The *New Yorker* magazine singled out one tune, "Honeysuckle Rose," as "a jazz vocal that is just about perfect." Anita sang the same lines several times, but changed the phrasing and the timing, throwing the listener off balance. By the final chorus, she was putting the accents in completely unlikely places: "WHEN I'm taking sips FROM your tasty lips SEEMS the honey fairly drips . . ." The man who wrote the lyrics, Andy Razaf, told her it was his favorite recording of the number. "He was especially high on my phrasing, elongating the first syllable of 'Honnnnnnnn-eee,'" Anita said.

"As news about *Anita* spread, everybody started welcoming me back. I felt like a kid again, back in the days when I'd walked along Broadway after making 'Let Me Off Uptown' and everybody was saying, 'Hi, Anita,' 'Hi, Anita.'"

From the first record to the expiration of her contract eight years later, Anita made fourteen albums with Verve, receiving $100,000 for the lot, plus $50 per song. That gave her an income (from recording) of roughly $13,500 a year at a time when a schoolteacher earned $4,000 annually. It was not a princely sum, but Anita no longer cared about money. "I just wanted to be able to sing my songs and have enough money to keep my [drug] habit supplied," she said.

Additional income came from touring, which Anita did frequently during "the Verve years." She traveled to New York with Louis Armstrong and vibraphonist Lionel Hampton; to Hollywood, California, with pianist Count Basie and pianist Oscar Peterson's trio; to Sweden and Germany with the Benny Goodman Orchestra (he decided he wanted "the girl who didn't sing the melody" after all) and, several times, to Japan.

When she was not on tour, Anita lived mostly in cheap hotels and friends' spare rooms. Her drifter lifestyle could hardly have been more atypical for the 1950s. The goal for most American women at the time was to marry, raise a family, and maintain a house. After World War II, the economy was strong and people had enough money to build new

What's New?

Stereo Records

The first stereo LP (long-playing) records were put on the market in 1957, enabling a listener to hear music through two channels of sound instead of one. Manufacturers designed special cabinets for the twin speakers and phonograph that were guaranteed "to blend perfectly with your lovely furniture."

Records, whether 45s or LPs, stereo or not, have a special importance for jazz. Because the music is not written down for the most part, musicians learn jazz by ear from other musicians. As trumpet player Dizzy Gillespie said, in jazz "each musician is based on someone who went before." The medium for learning who went before was—and is—recordings. Saxophonist Lester Young copied various horn players from records in order to decide whom he wanted to sound like. Anita O'Day admitted openly to imitating Billie Holiday's style after hearing her records.

An alternative to the transistor radio was the portable "stereo hi-fi" (high fidelity) record player, seen here in a Sears Catalog from 1961.

(SEARS ROEBUCK AND CO., PHILADELPHIA, PA)

Cut $**20** Portable Stereo Hi-fi with FM-AM Radio!

Now only $**129**⁹⁵ $5 down

homes, with a yard and a garage, in the suburbs that were developing outside of big cities to accommodate young families. Even college educated women were expected to become housewives, and to follow the advice in the women's magazines. "The two big steps that women must take are to help their husbands decide where they are going and use their pretty heads to help them get there," wrote Mrs. Dale Carnegie in the April 1955 issue of *Better Homes and Gardens.* Anita, on the other hand, married and divorced twice (the second time to Carl Hoff, a golf pro who was also her manager) and had no children. She didn't know how to cook or clean. When she sang, "If I am fancy free and love to wander, it's just the gypsy in my soul," she meant it. Anita traveled her own road.

She was on a largely destructive path, however. "If you saw me in Chicago, San Francisco, Milwaukee, Salt Lake City, wherever, during the Verve years I was on about the same trip. A lot of times I was higher than a kite. It didn't interfere with my singing as long as I got a good fix." There's no telling what kind of singer Anita might have been had she not spent all her time, money, and energy on her drug habit, whether it was getting dope or fleeing from the police. She'd arrive in a city, look in the newspaper to see what musicians were playing where, recognize the addicts, catch a performance by one of them, and almost invariably meet his or her "connection," or dealer. In the top New York City jazz club Birdland, the dealer could be found in the men's room with his packages laid out in full view on the windowsill. The Village Vanguard, another premier spot in Manhattan, was even more accommodating; it had a little room the size of a closet behind the stage where musicians cooked up dope and got their fix before going onstage.

Anita's constant companion in the late 1950s was John Poole, her drummer friend who had introduced her to heroin in 1954. "We were spending ten to twelve hours a day looking for [heroin] and playing games. I couldn't guess how much we spent on cosmetics I'd never wear and sundries John would never use just so we could add, 'Oh yes, and hypodermic needles for my vitamin shots.' It was hilarious. Who did we think we were fooling?"

The games ended for Anita when she overdosed on heroin in a ladies' rest room in Los Angeles on March 4, 1968. Fortunately, the friend who had supplied the drug found Anita unconscious and got her to a hospital, where a doctor jump-started her heart. When she recovered, the drug police were looking for her. She hocked her television set for plane fare and flew to Hawaii, where John Poole was living. He had kicked his own drug habit and encouraged Anita to do likewise, with his help. It took four agonizing months, but she finally succeeded.

What's New?

Transistor Radio

The year 1954 saw the first portable "transistor" radio, powered by small batteries. By 1957 the Sony Company was making a transistor radio that was small enough to fit into a shirt pocket or the palm of a hand. For the first time young people, the transistor radio's major users, had portable sound, which meant they could listen to music of their own choosing, not their parents'. The pocket-sized radio contributed to the rise of rock and roll and the development of Top 40 radio programming.

Save $3

Tiny 6-transistor
Shirt-pocket
Radio

Only $15⁹⁵

Not much bigger than a cigarette pack—yet this mighty midget speaks up big! Reaches stations miles away . . plays up to 90 hours on a mercury battery with amazingly clear tone.
Nonbreakable Dur-Pac plastic . . gold-color trim . About 2⅝x4x1 inches. 2¼-in. speaker. Earphone jack for private listening. Order battery, earphone and case separately.
Shpg. wt. 1 lb. *Was $18.95*.

57 X 1202—Black
57 X 1203—Mint green . . $15.95
57 X 6417—60-hour Standard battery. Shpg. wt. 4 oz . . . . . .79¢
57 X 6416—90-hour Mercury Battery. Shpg. wt. 6 oz $1.65
57 X 6507—Tan leather Case
Shipping weight 4 oz . . . . . . 89¢
57 X 6500—Earphone*.
Shipping weight 4 oz $1.49
*Earphones from Japan

Teenagers were the principal buyers of transistor radios, which cost just $15.95 when ordered from the Sears Catalog. The tiny portable machines enabled young people to listen to their own music at any time, something they had never been able to do before.

(SEARS ROEBUCK AND CO., PHILADELPHIA, PA)

★ Wearing a man's jacket, a skirt, and white blouse instead of the usual ball gown, Anita revolutionized the girl singer's wardrobe while she was with the Gene Krupa Band in the 1940s. *"I dodged dresses whenever possible. My uniforms became a kind of trademark and were eventually copied by a lot of band singers on tour."*

★ For traveling on the bus, Anita opted for kneesocks instead of a garter belt and silk stockings, which most women wore but which were scarce during World War II because the military needed all of the silk to make parachutes. (Nylon stockings had just been introduced—in 1940—when the military took over production of nylon, too. Nobody had even thought of pantyhose yet—they came on the market in 1959.)

★ A well-dressed woman never went out of the house without a hat in the 1950s, so Anita, singing at the Newport Jazz Festival, wore a big black cartwheel hat festooned with white feathers around the brim, which set off nicely a black sheath that ended just below the knee in a jaunty white ruffle, see-through plastic high-heeled shoes, and short white gloves.

★ On a television special called *Ford Startime: The Swinging Years in 1960*, Anita wore a hot pink dress (a short circle skirt over a matching sheath) and styled her brown hair in a flip. She held a black derby hat in her white-gloved hand.

★ For her 1989 performance at Michael's Pub, in New York City, she appeared in black slacks, a sparkling gold lamé jacket, and she wore no jewelry except a wristwatch. At nearly seventy, she was still "dodging dresses."

In 1969 Anita happened to share a New York City apartment briefly with Judy Garland, who was taking lots of pills and drinking heavily, and who Anita thought looked like "one of the walking dead." When Judy died shortly thereafter, Anita took the news as a warning. "I was . . . reminded to go right on telling hypes who were always offering me 'a little taste' that I wanted to pass. . . . Judy's death reinforced my determination to keep away from all that street stuff."

Anita continued to sing in clubs and to record, this time with her own company, Emily Records, named after her Yorkshire terrier. In 1975, a newspaper reported that Anita was working in Los Angeles-area clubs and living in a three dollar-a-day hotel room with no phone. "It was no big deal," she said. "In my time, I'd slept in worse places." Where Anita hangs her hat has never mattered; she cares only about what kind of music she makes. "When I'm up there with my rhythm section, improvising as the fourth musician in the combo, that's the time when I'm happiest," she says.

Anita wrote an engaging, tell-all autobiography, *High Times, Hard Times* (1981), which caused a surge in her popularity. Her recordings were reissued on CD, and she got better engagements, such as a several-weeks-long job at Michael's Pub in New York City in 1989. She was nearly seventy, and her voice was so small and worn that at times it was inaudible. Still, she poured so much music into the room that it was disappointing when she quit with a casual "bye" after just forty minutes. She took the word "stay," in "My Funny Valentine," on a wild ride, her voice climbing and dropping, darting, limping, disappearing, and reappearing. A *New York Times* critic called her "the best jazz singer performing today."

In the late 1990s, she suffered a series of illnesses that nearly killed her, but she bounced back, literally, deciding one day to get up out of her wheelchair and walk. Soon she was singing again, making weekly appearances in a Los Angeles supper club in 1999. She lived in a retirement home. Although she could no longer drive, she kept her car parked outside her window. She liked to go out and sit in the car—a symbol, perhaps, of the gypsy that remained in her soul.

Joan Baez
performing in
1970. Social
and music critic
Nat Hentoff
called her "an
imperfect
soldier in the
tiny army of the
actively
nonviolent."

JOAN BAEZ

Sibyl with Guitar

I N 1964 Joan Baez decided not to pay the portion of her annual federal income taxes that went toward building weapons. She wrote a letter to the American government:

Dear Friends:

What I have to say is this:

I do not believe in war. . . .

I am not going to volunteer the 60% of my year's income tax that goes to armaments. There are two reasons for my action. One is enough. It is enough to say that no man has the right to take another man's life. . . . My other reason is that modern war is impractical and stupid. We spend billions of dollars a year on weapons which scientists, politicians, military men, and even presidents all agree must never be used. . . .

Sincerely yours,
Joan C. Baez

Although she was only twenty-three years old, Joan was already famous as a folksinger, and when she released the letter to the press, it was printed around the world. By sending representatives to Joan's concerts to collect money from the cash register during performances, the government eventually got its tax money. But Joan didn't care: "The point was that I was refusing to give it to them and that they were spending a lot of time and money to come and collect it. And meanwhile, the tax resistance movement was growing."

Blessed with a thrilling, clear soprano voice, Joan realized early on that she could do more than sing. She could use her fame as a singer to draw attention to causes that were important to her.

Joan was absolutely right for her time. The 1960s was the age of protests, marches, and boycotts—and also eruptions of violence. Race riots destroyed whole sections of major cities. "Negroes" demanded to be called "blacks" in the 1960s, as they fought for such basic rights as voting and sitting where they wanted to on a bus. America's involvement in the Vietnam War—the longest and most unpopular war in American history—began in 1954 and escalated in the 60s, giving rise to a huge antiwar movement all over the country. Joan was active in all of these struggles, except the violent ones.

Joan had the good fortune to start out just as folk music was taking the country by storm. Folk music was a quieter, more contemplative alternative to rock and roll, and many folk songs carried a message, especially a political message, that appealed to a nation that was questioning long-held values and beliefs. Young people—teenagers and college students—in particular were drawn to folk songs recorded by singer-guitarists like Pete Seeger and the trio Peter, Paul, and Mary. Folk-music clubs sprang up in all of the big cities, and "folkies" congregated in the clubs and in places like Washington Square in New York City, to learn from each other new picking and strumming techniques and tunes.

Joan sang old folk ballads like "Geordie," about a young woman whose lover is to be hanged, and "Copper Kettle," about the pleasures of making moonshine. Later she added songs with political messages, like "Joe Hill," about a union organizer.

In the 1960s young people looking for causes and issues to wrap themselves up in were moved by this earnest young woman, her voice, and her physical presence. There was a startling purity about Joan: a dark-haired, dark-skinned beauty who wore simple clothes and often went barefoot. Her voice was as clear, sweet, and natural. Joan raised their consciousness and, sometimes, moved them to action. Out of the thousands of "girls with guitars," it was Joan, a friend of the Reverend Dr. Martin Luther King, Jr., who got to sing "We Shall Overcome" at the famous March on Washington for Jobs and Freedom when she was twenty-two. During the Vietnam War, young men turned in their draft cards to Joan, at her concerts.

Joan Baez was born on January 9, 1941, on Staten Island, New York, the second of three girls. Her father was Mexican, and her mother was Scottish; they had emigrated to the United States at an early age. The family moved frequently—ten times before Joan was eighteen—as her father, a physicist, sought research and teaching jobs. At one point, when he was undecided about whether or not to continue working in a job that involved testing fighter jets, the family became Quakers, a religious group known for its pacifism. In her biography, Joan called Quaker Meeting, the hour of silence that serves as a religious service, "a horror," and remembers

Joan Baez, with her brilliant smile, in the 1960s.
(MUSIC DIVISION. THE NEW YORK PUBLIC LIBRARY FOR THE PERFORMING ARTS, ASTOR, LENOX AND TILDEN FOUNDATIONS)

"the depressing tedium of silence broken only by tummy-rumbling, throat-clearing, and an occasional message from someone whom 'the spirit' had moved to speak." But it was through Quakerism that she first learned about alternatives to violence.

Joan was aware of injustices at an early age. In the fourth grade, she raised thirteen dollars from friends and their parents to buy a new dress, shoes, socks, and a hair ribbon for the poorest girl in her class. A year later, when Joan's family moved to Baghdad, Iraq, she became deeply disturbed when she saw animals beaten to death and children without legs dragging their fly-covered bodies along the street on cardboard, begging for money.

Joan felt the sting of prejudice herself when her family settled in Redlands, California. The local Mexican children wouldn't accept her because, although she looked Mexican, she didn't speak Spanish. The "Anglos" wouldn't have anything to do with her, either, because of her dark skin. She felt isolated in junior high school not only because of her ethnic background, but for other reasons as well. One was her beliefs: Joan was opposed to armaments at a time, the 1950s, when the United States was actively building up its defense system against the Soviet Union (which was in turn arming itself against the States). Another reason was that her experience of the world was, due to her travels, wider than that of her fellow students. In short, Joan felt different from everyone: "I was Joanie Boney, an awkward stringbean, fifteen pounds underweight, my hair a bunch of black straw whacked off just below my ears . . . my collar cockeyed, my scarf unmatched and wrinkled, my blouse too big, my

What's New?

Portable Record Players and Home Stereos

Young people were buying 45s by the dozen (they cost ninety-eight cents apiece) and playing them on inexpensive, portable players, which were made of plastic or "wipe-clean leatherette" and cost less than thirty dollars.

Their parents, meanwhile, purchased "home stereos," built to take advantage of the new stereo LP records ($4.98 each). The stereo consisted of three components: a turntable, which could play LPs, 78s, or 45s, and two speakers. The cost: about $175 to $300.

Cassette Player

Machines that played small music tapes called "cassettes" became available in the mid-60s. Initially the cassette player weighed about three pounds, and was powered by flashlight batteries. By 1968 it was small enough to fit in a shirt pocket.

socks belled, my shoes scuffed, my lunch bag many times used and crumpled, lines under my eyes and no lipstick."

Music, Joan discovered, eased her sense of isolation. When she was about thirteen years old, she taught herself four chords on a ukulele, sang requests during recess, and found instant popularity.

Joan figured out how to sing with "vibrato" by wiggling her finger up and down on the front of her neck, then imitating the "wobble" sound without using her finger. With her newfound voice, she got a spot in the high school talent show singing a popular rock-and-roll song by The Drifters, called "Honey Love." Although she did not win top prize, the audience asked for an encore. "For all the anxiety, I knew I'd been really good and that, in some strange way, my peers loved me and were proudly claiming me as one of their own," Joan recalled.

Joan was particularly drawn to folk music, especially Pete Seeger's and Odetta's songs, which she learned from records. Meanwhile, her social conscience was growing. When she was in eleventh grade, Joan attended a conference on world issues with a Quaker group, and encountered a twenty-seven-year-old black preacher, Martin Luther King, Jr. He talked about specific acts that could be done to fight injustice in America: refusing to ride buses that required blacks and whites to sit in separate sections; marching in "freedom walks" in the South, to protest civil rights violations; and organizing a nonviolent revolution. "When he finished his speech, I was on my feet, cheering and crying: King was giving a shape and a name to my passionate and ill-articulated beliefs."

After Joan graduated from high school, her family moved again, to Boston, where she enrolled at Boston University as a drama student. One night her father took the family to tiny, smoky, packed Tulla's Coffee Grinder in nearby Cambridge. Surrounded by serious conversation over coffee and the sound of a man playing classical guitar, Joan felt she had come "home."

Coffeehouses were a new phenomenon in American cities large and small in the late 1950s and early 1960s: small hole-in-the-wall restaurants that served no alcohol and offered live music—usually a singer with a guitar. They fueled the folk-music revival in Boston, San Francisco, and New York City's Greenwich Village. Joan immediately made friends with people who played guitars and sang, and spent most of her time learning traditional folk songs—"All My Trials," "John Riley," "Black Is the Color"—and how to play the guitar correctly. Consciously or not, she was following what Pete Seeger called "the folk process," learning and singing by ear, from untrained musicians, for fun, not for pay.

What Is a Folk Song?

A song that is not written down but is passed along from singer to singer, much as a folktale is passed from one storyteller to another, is generally called a folk song. The tune and words of a song can vary greatly according to the needs, mood, time, and place of the singer. A pop song, in contrast, is set, via either sheet music or sound recording, and changes little from singer to singer.

Big Bill Broonzy, an old-time blues singer, had his own definition: "I guess all songs is folksongs. I never heard no horse sing 'em."

When she was eighteen years old, Joan fell in love with a student from Trinidad, Michael New. Joan dropped out of college and got a job singing every Tuesday night at Club Mt. Auburn 47. It was a jazz coffeehouse that had never hired a folksinger before. Her nightly pay was ten dollars, which at the time could buy the simple skirt, blouse, and flat shoes she performed in. The first Tuesday, she sang for family and friends. Her second week, the club was half-filled, and from then on there were lines of people to hear Joan sing every Tuesday night. No longer an "awkward stringbean," Joan had grown into an exotic-looking young woman with a brilliant smile. She mesmerized people with sad ballads like "Go 'Way From My Window." She liked to remove her shoes, which revealed her slender feet. If she seemed aloof, it was because inside she was terrified.

"She could be very difficult, very arrogant, rude, hysterical—she had stage fright half the time," one of Club 47's owners recalled. "She used to go out in the alley and throw up, she was so scared."

Stage fright and other insecurities tormented Joan for many years. She worked hard to quell her anxieties, and even entered psychoanalysis in her twenties. She never canceled a performance, but she often required assistance from an understanding person—her mother or sister Mimi or a boyfriend—before and sometimes after a show.

When an older folksinger-friend, Bob Gibson, invited Joan to the Newport Folk Festival in 1959, she was "petrified." The festival marked her first important singing engagement, and she caused a great sensation when she performed two songs with Gibson. "There was something about her voice as it floated out on the night air, singing these beautiful strange songs that left you speechless," recalled one listener. "She was so young and looked so vulnerable in a simple dress and her bare feet, but her voice had power in it to chill you to the bone."

In part as a result of her success at the folk festival, the recording companies Columbia and Vanguard came forward with contracts. Joan chose to sign with the less prestigious, more serious Vanguard, and made her first record album (*Joan Baez*) in 1960. But just as the album sales took off (to number three among the top one hundred albums in the country), Joan dropped out of the folk-music scene and went to live in a one-room cabin in California with Michael New. He resented her fame and was dismissive

Joan Baez performing with Bob Dylan in 1964.
(LIBRARY OF CONGRESS, *LOOK* MAGAZINE PHOTOGRAPH COLLECTION. DOUGLAS R. GILBERT, PHOTOGRAPHER)

of her career, but fortunately for Joan, her career was moving too fast for her to stop it now. She hired a manager, who kept her performing and making records at a rate of one a year for twelve years. She saw her portrait on the cover of *Time* magazine, while inside the article carried the headline SIBYL WITH GUITAR. "Her voice is as clear as air in the autumn, a vibrant, strong, untrained and thrilling soprano. She wears no makeup, and her long black hair hangs like a drapery, parted around her long almond face. . . . Impressarios everywhere are trying to book her." Joan was only twenty-one years old.

She tired of Michael New and their cut-off-from-the-world existence, and left him, hoping to be able to integrate better her life and her beliefs with her singing. In New York City she met Bob Dylan. He looked forlorn in a worn, too-small leather jacket, and he sang his own songs in a crusty, creaky voice. Joan fell in love. Many years later she wrote a hauntingly

WHAT JOAN WORE

★ In the coffeehouses around 1959, Joan wore a prim white blouse, a dark circle skirt to just past the knee, and flat shoes. She wore her hair long and straight, in sharp contrast to the style of the day, the "bouffant," short hair teased with a comb into looking high and poofy.

★ For her first appearance at the Newport Folk Festival in 1959, Joan made a splash in a bright orange knit and crocheted "rebozo," a long Mexican shawl lined in silk—*"the fanciest bit of clothing I'd ever worn onstage"*—and "gladiator sandals" with thongs that laced up to just below the knee.

★ Her concert dress around 1963 was a simple dress, necklace, and bare feet. *"The effect was Biblical but gloomy."*

★ For her wedding in New York City in March 1968 she wore a Grecian-style, off-white floor-length dress and no shoes.

★ In the 1970s Joan wore expensive suits from I. Magnin and Saks Fifth Avenue, but she felt guilty about having nice things when the world was full of people who had little. *"I try to ease the guilt by getting four of one outfit and giving three away."*

★ To open the Live-Aid concert in 1985, an international event to ease a horrific famine in Ethiopia, she chose a flowing, yellow silk skirt, a cobalt blue blouse, a leather belt with big silver medallions, a necklace made of spoons, and black sandals studded with rhinestones. Her hair was cropped short.

beautiful song called "Diamonds & Rust" that captured her feelings at the time: She called Dylan "a legend, the unwashed phenomenon, the original vagabond" who strayed into her arms.

Joan and Dylan toured together and met the Beatles together in 1965, and he wrote a love song for her, "Farewell Angelina," with cryptic, imaginative lyrics about machine guns and puppets eating rust, time bombs and elves dancing on rooftops.

"Bob's songs seemed to update the concepts of justice and injustice," Joan said. "Nothing could have spoken better for our generation than [Dylan's song] 'The Times They Are A-Changin'.' The civil rights movement was in full bloom, and the war which would tear this nation asunder, divide, wound and irreparably scar millions upon millions of people was moving toward us like a mighty storm."

As a couple, though, Joan and Dylan were ultimately ill-matched. "I asked him what made us different, and he said it was simple, that I thought I could change things, and he knew that no one could."

Joan joined Dr. King in the South in 1963, helping to register black children in all-white schools, and in Washington, D.C., marching for civil rights for black people. There, on an August afternoon, Dr. King abandoned his notes and launched into the now-famous, spontaneous speech, "I have a dream . . . ," and Joan led the marchers in "We Shall Overcome." "My knees were knocking," she called. "I was so young, and it was such a big crowd, 250,000 people."

In 1965, the United States increased its involvement in the Vietnam War, and Joan sang at the first antiwar march on Washington, in April, which drew only twenty-five thousand protesters. She wrote to her parents, "I want to start a peace movement," having no notion of what it might consist. It turned out to be a school. Joan bought the house and land herself, in Carmel, California, and opened the Institute for the Study of Non-Violence. An old friend, Ira Sandperl, did most of the teaching. Joan and other young men and women studied the teachings and writings of pacifist Indian Prime Minister Mahatma Gandhi and meditated. Although she still performed about twenty concerts a year in the United States, music now took a backseat to Joan's activism.

There was much cause for action. During the summers of 1965 to 1968, race riots erupted in more than one hundred American cities in protest against generations of injustice against black people. Two Presidents, Lyndon B. Johnson and Richard Nixon, campaigned on a promise of peace in Vietnam, only to escalate the war once elected. By 1968 the United States had more than 500,000 troops there. At home an antiwar movement was going strong. All eighteen-year-old men were required to register for the draft, which supplied most of the troops, but some 250,000 men refused. Another 110,000 men burned their draft cards.

Joan participated in "sit-in" demonstrations (sitting in the building and refusing to leave at closing time) at a California draft center, and got arrested twice. One of her visitors in jail was David Harris, a popular speaker in the antiwar movement and a draft dodger. "He cared about little kids dying under our bombs in Vietnam, and sometimes all I could think about was those kids," she said. They fell in love and were married in March 1968. They toured colleges as an antiwar duo—he spoke and she sang—and lived in a commune they called Struggle Mountain, in California. They were "hippies," eating vegetables and no meat and "doing their own thing." Joan embraced hippie culture in all but one aspect: She didn't use drugs. "I don't think there's a shortcut to enlightenment," she said.

In the summer of 1969, Harris got word that he was going to be arrested for avoiding the draft, and fellow pacifists gathered in his and Joan's front yard to await the event. Joan "spent the days baking bread and making pancakes and fruit salads for endless numbers of friends and well-wishers." Finally, on July 15, the sheriff arrived and arrested Harris. As the sheriff drove off with his prisoner, Joan and her friends got a laugh from the RESIST THE DRAFT bumper sticker someone had plastered on the patrol car.

Harris's twenty-month prison term was, in a way, a stimulating and satisfying time for Joan. She felt close to Harris, united as they were in spirit, and Joan continued to be active in the peace movement. She finished making a movie they had been filming about the war resistance and took the movie on a tour of college campuses, calling herself a "nonviolent soldier." In December 1969 she gave birth to their son, Gabriel.

One can understand just how intensely Joan was living by listening to an interview with her in 1970. "Music *alone* isn't enough for me," she said. "If I'm not on the side of life in action as well as in music, then all those sounds, however beautiful, are irrelevant to the only real question of this century: How do we stop men from murdering each other, and what am I doing with my life to help stop the murdering? Whatever I do now in music has to be part of that larger context."

Sadly, Joan's marriage did not survive Harris's release from prison in 1971. "I couldn't breathe, and I couldn't try anymore to be a wife," Joan said. They divorced and raised their son jointly. She has not remarried. "I am meant to live alone," she wrote in her autobiography.

Joan soldiered on. As part of a mission to keep some kind of friendly relations with the "enemy," Joan traveled with a small group of activists to North Vietnam in December 1972. Her timing could not have been worse: In the week before Christmas, President Nixon launched a devastating air attack that lasted twelve days. The attack is said to be the heaviest bombing in the history of the world. Joan spent the days viewing the

The Reverend Dr. Martin Luther King, Jr., speaking during the 1963 civil rights march in Washington, D.C. He delivered his "I Have a Dream" speech, and Joan Baez led the marchers in singing "We Shall Overcome."
(LIBRARY OF CONGRESS)

Protesters burning U.S. dollar bills to demonstrate their opposition to the American involvement in the Vietnam War. Joan Baez took part in many such protests.
(LIBRARY OF CONGRESS)

effects of the bombing and the nights in bomb shelters, quelling her own and others' fears with songs like "Kumbaya." She saw a bent-over woman beside a thirty-foot crater, hobbling back and forth and singing, "My son, my son. Where are you now, my son?" Joan crumpled to the ground and sobbed. "Such depths of sadness cannot exist," she wrote. When she got home she recorded an album, *Where Are You Now, My Son?* that she called "my gift to the Vietnamese people, and my prayer of thanks for being alive."

Joan's involvement in Southeast Asia did not end with the war's end in 1975. Four years later she published a highly controversial "Open Letter to the Socialist Republic of Vietnam" in five United States newspapers. The letter blasted the country's "brutal disregard of human rights," specifically the detaining, starving, and torturing of more than 150,000 Vietnamese political prisoners. As a result of her letter, many prisoners were released. Joan organized a concert at the Lincoln Memorial followed by a candlelight march to the White House, urging President Jimmy Carter to rescue Cambodian and Laotian refugees known as the "boat people." Later that night, the president announced that he was sending the Sixth Fleet to the South China Sea on a rescue mission.

In the 1980s Joan turned her considerable energies to a now-flailing music career. Her record sales had declined. Folk music had fallen completely out of fashion, pushed aside by disco and hard rock. Discovering that she was no longer "timely" was "painful and humilitating," she said, but she was determined to continue. She modified her style to a kind of folk-rock, hiring a band and writing her own songs or seeking excellent contemporary material from other songwriters. She recorded, toured the United States and, in 1983, traveled to Paris, where she performed a free concert dedicated to nonviolence, for a crowd of 100,000 people—and suffered terrible stage fright beforehand.

Joan consulted a vocal coach for the first time, who helped her to get back some of the high notes she had lost to age and who taught her how to warm up before a performance. In the 1990s her voice was no longer high and clear but deep and rich, and it still had that distinctive vibrato. She needed a good song, though, to make her mark, and occasionally she found one, like John Hiatt's "Through Your Hands," about how a simple gesture like helping someone can become a powerful agent for change. In Joan's voice—that voice of conviction that recalls a time when a great many people thought they could change the world—the song was like an oracle. "In time you will move mountains . . . ," she sang. Indeed she did.

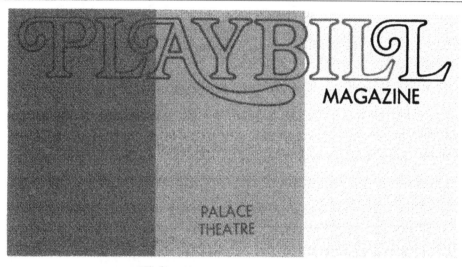

Program for Bette Midler at the Palace Theatre, December 1973.

DIEGO UCHITEL

BETTE MIDLER

The Last of the Real Tacky Ladies

REMEMBER AM RADIO?" Bette (pronounced "bet") Midler asked her audience at the Continental Baths, a gay men's club in New York City in 1970. "Oh, my dears, AM. That's where it was all at. You didn't have to think, just listen. What fabulous trash. The Shirelles, Gladys Knight and the Pips. Okay, I'll be the leader, you can be the Dixie Cups." Bette sang, ". . . 'Cause we're going to the chapel and we're gonna get ma-a-a-ried," and the men all joined in.

Everyone always sang along to the wonderfully schlocky "Chapel of Love" when Bette told them to. She drew audiences to her, and they, in turn, mobilized her. "Audiences just set me on fire," she said. "I feel I can do any old thing." And she did. She dressed up as a mermaid and whizzed around stage in a wheelchair, because mermaids can't walk, of course. She lay in the humongous hand of King Kong, gazed into his eyes, and sang, "Nicky Arnstein! Nicky Arnstein, Nicky Arnstein," sounding just like singer and actress Barbra Streisand crooning the name of her boyfriend in the movie *Funny Girl*. And Bette told bawdy jokes, many of them about her ample breasts, which she shook like a stripper.

If Bette had been born in Sophie Tucker's time, she would have been in vaudeville. She was equal parts singer, comedienne, and clown, and she came alive onstage. Instead, she started out in the 1970s, when rock music, disco dancing, and movies were the big entertainments. She didn't have

Bette Midler and her backup trio, the Harlettes.
(MICHAEL GILLESPIE COLLECTION)

the voice of a rock singer, so she carved her own path, combining pop music and theater, using the medium of cabaret. What began as a fairly simple act grew into an elaborate stage show with a band, backup singers, and fantastic props. And then, when she was in her forties, she embarked upon a second career in the movies.

Her accompanist in the early years, Barry Manilow, recalled their first performance together, at the Continental Baths in 1970, when she was twenty-five. Despite three rehearsals, Manilow was unprepared for the "whirling red-haired dynamo" who emerged from the dressing room. "She tore her way to the small stage in front of me and began singing 'Friends' in a way I hadn't heard her do in rehearsal," he recalled. "She shouted, she screamed, she kicked, she flailed her arms and legs. I found myself laughing hysterically at her outrageous jokes; during 'Am I Blue?' I welled up with emotion as she poured out her breaking heart . . . and at the end, when she sang 'I Shall Be Released,' I broke three piano strings pounding out the accompaniment to her fury. . . . I didn't expect her to be funny or filthy or dramatic and most of all I didn't expect her to be so musical." Bette had come alive onstage.

On that occasion, she wore a black lace corset, gold lamé pedal pushers, and platform shoes, her hair looking like she had stuck her finger in an electric socket. She wasn't "movie star" pretty at twenty-five, but she was sexy. Standing five feet one inch tall, with an oval face and a large nose, Bette was big-busted and went braless, a common choice in the 70s, when feminism was in full force and women objected to confinement of any sort. Bette had slim, shapely legs—all the better for skittering across the stage like a sandpiper—and a smile that was wide, toothy, and warm. "You know that satisfaction you get when you make a baby smile? It's like that," said Jerry Blatt, co-creator of her shows. "You and that smile have an intimate relationship."

Bette was born on December 1, 1945, in Honolulu, Hawaii. Her parents had moved there from New Jersey to start a new life in an exotic land. Bette's father worked as a housepainter for the U.S. Navy, and her mother was a housewife who loved the movies and read fan magazines. She named Bette after the movie star Bette Davis, pronouncing the name "bet" because she didn't know the actress pronounced her name "Betty." With her two older sisters, and a younger brother who was born mentally retarded, Bette felt isolated from other children because the Midler family was white and Jewish, while Bette's neighbors and schoolmates were Chinese, Samoan, Japanese, and Filipino, and, mostly, Christian. "I was an alien, a foreigner even though I was born there. I remember children being so cruel," Bette said. In first grade, when she won a prize for singing "Silent Night," she felt accepted. In fifth grade, she sang "Lullaby of Broadway" in a talent

Bette and "Camp"

Bette's act was often described as "camp" or "campy," words that are not easily understood. Susan Sontag, in a 1964 "Notes on Camp" essay, called camp a "sensibility" and "a vision of the world" containing "the love of the exaggerated" and "the spirit of extravagance." Bette Midler's act fits these definitions perfectly. The ultimate camp statement, Sontag said, is "it's good because it's awful." There *is* something awful about a family of mermaids in wheelchairs, but it's funny and entertaining as well.

On the other hand, Bette's work may not be "pure camp." As defined by Sontag, pure camp is unconscious; it does not mean to be funny. Bette most assuredly meant to be funny. So "campy" is probably a better description of Bette's style than "camp."

show, and the class voted her the best and gave her a two-dollar prize. "I'll never forget that flush of happiness," she said. Bette spent the rest of her school years performing whenever she could.

When she was twelve years old, a librarian gave her a ticket to a stage performance. "I looked up at the stage and there were all those shining people," Bette remembered. "They were dancing and singing, looking so happy. It was the most wonderful thing I'd ever seen."

In high school, Bette got caught up in the folksinging craze and formed a trio of folksingers called the Pieridine Three. She also won a statewide championship for dramatic interpretation and played the lead in the senior class play, *When Our Hearts Were Young and Gay*. She told a friend she wanted to become a performer and go to New York City, but after graduation she worked in a pineapple-canning factory, then enrolled as a drama student at the University of Hawaii. Two years later, Bette got a bit part in

What's New?

Recording Studio Revolution

In the studio, the 32-track recorder made it more possible than ever to edit tape. Now one musician could play all the musical instruments—one at a time, of course—and a producer would remix them together. Acoustic instruments were often replaced by a synthesizer, electronic keyboard, and a drum machine. Because it could provide a perfectly steady beat, the drum machine was important in the rise of disco, the seventies music-and-dance craze.

The "Boom Box" and the Walkman

The portable stereo cassette player, known as the "boom box," had the potential noise level of a jet engine. After the player came on the market in the 1970s, it was immediately popular among young people, who liked to carry boom boxes as they strolled the sidewalks. It became impossible to walk the streets of big cities without encountering the blare of recorded music.

In 1979 Sony introduced the Soundabout cassette player with tiny headphones for two hundred dollars, which became known as the Walkman. The price dropped until, ten years later, the Walkman cost $20 and nearly everyone owned one, just as they had a TV or radio. With its soft headphones and easy portability, the personal cassette player was useful in drowning out the noise of everyday life—including the sound of the boom box.

the movie *Hawaii*, a nonspeaking role that required her to vomit over the side of a boat. She saved her salary and pocketed sixty-eight dollars of the daily seventy-dollar allotment for food and essentials. When she had one thousand dollars in her purse, she flew to New York City to become a dramatic actress. She was twenty.

Bette got a room in a seedy hotel near the theater district, took acting, singing, and dancing classes, auditioned for parts, and worked in a variety of low-paying jobs, including typist, clerk, and hatcheck girl. For eight months in 1966 she tried to get a part in *Fiddler on the Roof*, which was the longest-running musical on Broadway to date. She finally got a spot in the chorus, and the following year the role of the oldest daughter, Tzeitel, who marries a poor tailor, which she played for three years.

One night after the show, she and a friend went to a smoky little bar called Hilly's, known as a place where aspiring singers could sing a few songs for no pay. When Bette's turn came, "she was very hesitant, kind of embarrassed," her friend recalled. The noisy room grew quiet for her three numbers. During the last, "God Bless the Child," she said, "Something happened to my head and my body, and it was just the most wonderful sensation I'd ever been through."

Overnight Bette became serious about singing. She pored over old songs at The New York Public Library for the Performing Arts. Her friend Ben Gillespie played records for her by Aretha Franklin, Tina Turner, and Bessie Smith. He took her to see Janis Joplin in concert. "He made me want to sing," Bette said.

The chance to sing came on Saturday nights at the Continental Baths, a club for gay men, with a swimming pool, bar, and dance floor. Bette's audience was thirty or so men dressed only in towels, and she was paid fifty dollars a night. At first, she simply sang. Then a friend, a writer named Bill Hennessey, encouraged her to "be insane." For her encores, *she* wore only a towel. The wilder she got, the more the audience loved it. She created a character, the Divine Miss M—"the last of the real tacky ladies"—who said vulgar things, and the men loved it. "As an audience, gay men are spectacular," she said. "They're not ashamed to show how they feel about you. They applaud like hell, they scream and carry on, stamp their feet and laugh." Bette's gay following would continue devotedly throughout her career.

In an age that coined the expression "let it all hang out," Bette fit well. The 1970s saw a new permissiveness in society. Rules were breaking down, and previously powerless groups gained authority: College students devised their own programs of study and lived in coed dormitories; the "feminist movement" inspired women to consider their needs, educate themselves, and get better jobs; homosexual people "came out of the closet" and revealed themselves as lesbians and gay men. People in the 1970s were still involved in causes, but the causes were often personal. Self-discovery became more important than changing the world. In another, more conservative era, Bette would probably not have succeeded. As it was, many people in the 1970s celebrated her individualism, just as they embraced their own.

A few months after her first pianist-arranger left and recommended Barry Manilow as a replacement, Bette's act found its musical center. Bette chose the songs, Manilow shaped them to suit her interpretations, and they argued fiercely. "We would mostly bicker about which song should go where and how the show should be paced, and whether he was going to wear white tails or not, and would he please stop waving his head," Bette said. "He would always want to know how come I was always half a tone under and why I didn't come in on time." She noted, however, that "He very rarely did an arrangement I didn't like." Bette and Manilow remained a team until 1973, when he left to pursue his own, and ultimately very successful, career as a singer.

Meanwhile, Bette was becoming known to an entirely different, much larger group of people via television, on the popular late-night talk program, *The Tonight Show*. Host Johnny Carson recognized the immense talent in this woman who could break your heart with a ballad and then, in the next moment, crack you up with her brassy, rapid-fire chatter.

"I've said it before, and I'll say it again: You're going to be something to contend with," Carson said to Bette on the show in 1972. "You're going to be a big star in this business. . . . When it all comes together, it'll happen."

Bette worked hard to make it come together. Acquaintances described her as driven. She would be in her apartment talking with friends, say, "Give me a minute," and walk away. She'd face the wall and run through her entire show in fast motion. Then she'd return to the conversation, saying, "All right, where were we?"

When she opened at her first real nightclub, Downstairs at the Upstairs, nobody came. Bette placed an ad in *Screw* magazine, announcing to her gay audience: "Bette from the Baths at the Downstairs." As soon as the ad appeared, the club was packed, and the club owner extended Bette's two-week engagement to two months.

"I wanted to be a phenomenon. I didn't want to be just a schlepper," Bette said, and the "phenomenon" came to fruition in 1972, after she hired manager Aaron Russo, who devoted himself obsessively to her career.

The 1970s saw a nostalgia trend, with people favoring clothes and music of the 1930s and '40s, in particular. Bette took the trend several steps further, choosing material of many periods and styles and tying it all together in one oversized, campy, fabulous bundle. She resurrected Bessie Smith's blues, the Andrews Sisters' "Boogie Woogie Bugle Boy" from World War II, and 1960s rock and roll. She did her own idiosyncratic interpretations of contemporary songs like "Delta Dawn," which was a big hit for Helen Reddy in 1973. The song is about a woman who is jilted by her man, who has promised to marry her but never shows. At first Bette is sympathetic to Delta Dawn, then she makes fun of her and, finally, identifies with her and her hopeless dreams.

Program for the *Clams on the Half Shell Revue*, New York City, April 1975.

(PLAYBILL® IS A REGISTERED TRADEMARK OF PLAYBILL, INC. ALL RIGHTS RESERVED. USED BY PERMISSION. MICHAEL GILLESPIE COLLECTION)

Bette Midler as Delores DeLago, a mermaid in a wheelchair, 1978.
(MICHAEL GILLESPIE COLLECTION)

"Music has to pick you up and throw you down again," Bette said.

Bette appeared atop a huge, glittery silver high-heeled shoe and descended the stairs built inside it while singing "Lullaby of Broadway" at the Palace Theatre, where Judy Garland had once been a smash. For Bette's song, "Chapel of Love," an oversized heart appeared behind her with the words of the song on it, and of course the audience sang along.

"There was something about the way Bette sang, 'Gee, I really love you and we're gonna get married' that made me want to hug her," wrote rock critic and radical feminist Ellen Willis in *The New Yorker*. "On one level she was indulging her joy in a simple-minded, happy rock-and-roll song. On another, she was saying, 'Gee, I really love you.' And I believed her; I even believed in marriage."

Other critics wrote of Bette's "great guileless smile," her "gaiety and sweetness," "astonishing range of new material," and "big, wrap-around voice." *Newsweek* noted an "unmistakable vulnerability" that lay beneath the kind of cocky attitude that made her ask, with a limp wrist and one hip thrust out, "Whose idea was it to play this dump?"—at the Palace. Underneath all the glitz and zaniness, Bette *was* vulnerable. "I was a very frightened person," she said—she was frightened of success, of failure, and of losing the affection of her cast and crew. Russo managed her career brilliantly, but fed her fears. He was a jealous, manipulative man who told Bette that everyone was against her except him, thereby creating terrific tension backstage. He and Bette fought at least once a day.

Still, Bette managed to put together a new, extravagant stage show almost every year throughout the 1970s. "I had a lot of things to say, so I had to find vehicles to say them," she said. She enlisted the help of writers, occasionally a director, musicians, and a female backup trio called the Harlettes. She created new stage characters including Vicki Eydie (pronounced ee-dee), who was a lounge singer (i.e., a not-very-good singer), "trapped in an act not of her own design," the star of a revue called Around the World in Eighty Ways. Vicki evolved into Delores DeLago, the Toast of Chicago, a mermaid in a wheelchair. She was a lounge singer *and* a Polynesian poi-ball twirler at the same time.

Bette's jokes, which sounded so spontaneous onstage, were the result of hours and hours of work. Said comedy writer Bruce Vilanch: "Bill [Hennessey] and I would write up pages and pages for her, and then she'd sit there curled up in a little ball with her blue pencil and write 'No!' next to everything she didn't like, and then the three of us would rewrite together. She made *major* contributions."

Here's Bette talking to an audience in Passaic, New Jersey, in 1971: "Well I missed my stop on the Seventh Avenue and wound up here in Passaic." She pauses to primp her hair. "Passaic, darling, I do not *believe*. Honey, I never saw so many women in curlers in my life! I want you all to know we are embarking on a tour of the tackiest towns in America—and Passaic is definitely *numero uno!*" Bette, of course, called herself the tacky Divine Miss M, so her criticism did not sting, but amuse.

WHAT BETTE WORE

★ In about 1969, in a thrift shop, Bette found a long black velvet gown with beaded sleeves for ten dollars (one-tenth the cost of a designer dress). The gown reminded her of torch singer Helen Morgan, and set Bette off on a lifelong love affair with costumes.

★ Wearing only a diaper, and a white sash across her chest that read *1973*, Bette sang "Auld Lang Syne" to ring in the new year at New York's Philharmonic Hall.

★ In white slacks, a loud Hawaiian shirt, and a lei, Bette opened her show at the Palace Theatre in 1973, singing "Friends."

★ As Delores DeLago, she wore a spangly silver and black mermaid skirt with a tail, and a black bra decorated with two gold starfish.

She made some unusual hats for public appearances:

★ At a book signing (*A View from a Broad*) in Los Angeles, a jet plane and globe on a cloud of net fabric. At the New York signing, a typewriter on net. *"All lady authors should wear hats."*

★ A 45 rpm record, for the 1975 Grammy Awards ceremony. *"It's 'Come Go with Me' by the Del Vikings. A great record but a better hat."*

★ At home in the 1990s, Bette padded around in tight black cotton leggings and two large gray sweaters. *"I wouldn't be caught dead with a sequin on my body when I'm not working. How* tasteless.*"*

Manager Russo, meanwhile, was not satisfied with a national tour, a Tony Award (for the Palace run), and a Grammy Award for Best New Artist after Bette's first album, *The Divine Miss M.* He felt that Bette couldn't be a true "legend" unless she was in movies. The film he found for her was *The Rose*, about a self-destructive rock star, loosely based on Janis Joplin, who died of a drug overdose. Bette took to the script immediately. She understood Rose's world and, like Rose, had a domineering, manipulative manager. Bette also loved rock music: "It's loud and screechy and my favorite kind of music." She sang the concert scenes before live audiences, who were told to "dress 1969" and scream for "The Rose," not "Bette." She didn't sound like a rock singer, but she looked like one. "What a storm of acting!" gushed *New York Magazine* at the movie's release in 1979.

By then, Russo was gone. Bette had fired him at the end of 1978, saying, "I outgrew my need for drama." Unfortunately, because Russo had done so much and Bette had been so dependent on him, she discovered she knew almost nothing about the entertainment business. In a television interview in 1980, looking exhausted and distressed, Bette told Barbara Walters, "I'm very close to falling apart." But she didn't. An agonizing seven years passed between *The Rose* and her next successful movie, but Bette slowly took control of her own career. In 1980 she published an autobiographical book, *A View from a Broad,* which was full of jokes and bawdy stories from a world concert tour she took in 1978. In 1982 Bette assembled a completely new road show, De Tour, which featured the entire DeLago family,

Bette Midler as she appeared on her 1998 *Bathhouse Betty* album.
(WARNER BROS. RECORDS INC.)

four mermaids in a wheelchair ballet, singing the Sister Sledge song "We Are Family," and a joke about weighing her breasts on a postal scale: "I won't tell you how much they weighed, but it costs eighty-seven dollars and fifty cents to send them to Brazil!" She formed her own movie production company with two women partners, All Girl Productions ("our motto: we hold a grudge").

Along the way she met a nice, eccentric man, Martin von Haselberg, a commodities trader and performance artist, half of a duo called the Kipper Kids, known for doing goofy things like throwing pudding at each other. After dating for less than three months, they drove to Las Vegas and were married in an all-night chapel on December 16, 1984. On the drive home to Los Angeles they were "fairly shaken," she recalled. "We went there on a lark, and now it was going to be real."

Marriage seemed to calm and soothe Bette. "He is so stabilizing," she said of her husband. In 1986, they had a daughter, Sophie.

With her husband's encouragement, Bette began to make more movies, first as a comedienne (in *Ruthless People* and others) and then, fulfilling the goal she'd had since she was twenty, as a dramatic actress

What is Cabaret?

The room is small, the lights are low, and the tables are close to one another. People sip their drinks and listen; talk is minimal. The stage is so close, you can see every bead on the singer's gown, every change in facial expression, the sheen of her stockings when she sits atop the piano for a "torch song"—an emotional ballad, usually about love. The feeling is so intimate, you feel she's doing a show for just you. An hour passes swiftly. Then the lights come up. The mood is broken. You're sitting at a table scattered with empty glasses, in a room full of people.

That's cabaret.

Bette started out in cabaret, which people like Mabel Mercer had made popular in the 1950s. Barbra Streisand also began her career in nightclubs, in 1961. By 1970, though, cabaret was dying out. Bette's appearances at New York City clubs like the Improv, Downstairs at the Upstairs, and the Bitter End helped resurrect the scene, along with the 1972 movie *Cabaret*, starring Judy Garland's daughter Liza Minnelli. The club Reno Sweeney (named for the character created by Ethel Merman in the show *Anything Goes*) was a favorite haunt of the less well-heeled. It opened in late 1972, just when Bette was starting to hit the big-time, and though she never performed there, she went frequently and sat under a soft, hidden spotlight at table D-5, which was reserved for celebrities.

(in *Beaches*, a TV version of *Gypsy*, and *The First Wives Club*, among others).

Busy on stage and screen, Bette had paid minimal attention to her recording career. The success of two singles, "Wind Beneath My Wings" and "From a Distance," aside, she had become frustrated by the recording process and the record business. Her habit of singing out of tune, which might go unnoticed in a live performance, stood out on recording. Atlantic, her record company, seemed not to know what to do with such a diverse performer.

Around 1995, Bette began to turn the situation around. She worked on her vocal technique, and as a result she could sing more notes and more in tune. She signed a contract with Warner Bros. record company and recorded *Bathhouse Betty* in 1998. It had a little bit of everything: old songs, hip new songs, funny songs, and heartbreaker ballads. Her voice was controlled, warm, and easy. The contemporary rhythm-and-blues song "I'm Beautiful" seemed to capture her fiercely defiant attitude at the age of fifty-three: "Rise up and repeat after me: 'I'm beautiful, damn it!'"

"Bette simply seems so real," the choreographer and composer Meredith Monk said. The "realness" of Bette is what comes through in no matter what she does, whether it's singing or acting, recorded or live, ragged or polished smooth—or saying good-bye to Johnny Carson, who had chosen her to be a guest for his penultimate *Tonight Show*, in 1992.

"Do you like my outfit?" Bette asked, wearing an absurd black swinging baby-doll dress with chartreuse flowers stuck all over it.

"I think it's—yes, yes, I do. It's a—fashion statement," Carson stammered.

"It was the last one out of Frederick's of Hollywood [a store famous for sexy, tacky lingerie] before they torched it."

She sang "One for My Baby (And One More for the Road)," sitting on a high stool, facing Carson. They gazed at each other with gratitude: He for being honored on an important occasion, she for having been recognized by him thirty years earlier when she was a nobody. "You may not know it, but buddy, you're a kind of poet," she sang gently, ending quietly, "Thanks for the cheer." She placed an orange lei around Carson's neck and walked off the set. Very classy, very Bette. So real.

Mid-1980s
Madonna: dyed
blond hair, and
wrists loaded
with jewelry,
including the
black rubber O-
ring bracelets.
(MUSIC DIVISION, THE NEW
YORK PUBLIC LIBRARY FOR THE
PERFORMING ARTS, ASTOR,
LENOX AND TILDEN
FOUNDATIONS)

MADONNA

Material Girl

I N A VIDEO on MTV, Madonna was dancing in a strapless pink gown and telling a dozen men in tuxedos, "We are living in a material world, and I am a material girl." She stroked her mink stole, touched her diamond necklace, and caressed her silk-clad body. She flirted with the men; she flirted with the camera. The message was clear: The way to my heart, boys, is cash and lots of it.

It was 1984, and feminists were horrified by Madonna and that video in particular, saying she set women back thirty years. Madonna dismissed her critics with a wave of her gloved hand. "If they don't get the humor in me or my act, then they don't want to get it," she said.

Teenage girls got everything about Madonna, and they made up a large part of her audience. They came to her concerts in 1985 dressed like her, in black short skirts, and tops that exposed their belly buttons, wearing long necklaces, lots of rubber bracelets, and crucifix-shaped earrings, their hair tousled and tied with rags. "I like the way she handles herself, sort of take it or leave it," said one seventeen-year-old girl in Houston, Texas. "She's sexy but she doesn't need men. She's kind of there by herself."

Madonna was indeed by herself. No other female entertainer came close to achieving her fame, fortune, and influence in the 1980s. She wasn't a great singer or a great dancer, and she didn't have a picture-perfect body, but she made the most of what she had. Although her voice was

What's New?

Compact Disc

In 1982 a small plastic disc with a diameter of four and three-fourth inches brought about a revolution in sound technology. The compact disc, or CD, could hold up to seventy-five minutes of music, did not deteriorate with use, and had no extraneous noise: no hissing, popping, or humming. Six years later the CD surpassed the LP record in sales, and soon after, recording companies quit making records altogether. Instead, companies reissued the music on CD. The sound was so much better, and the disc so easy to handle, that people actually replaced their records with CDs containing the same music, at a cost of up to eighteen dollars a disc. (The use of the words "record" and "album," though, continued through the end of the century, as synonyms for CD.)

Not everyone jumped immediately onto the CD bandwagon, however. There were still an estimated 90 million turntables (for playing records) in use in 1991, as compared to 20 million CD players.

The real revolution, culturally speaking, came when recording companies began digging into their vaults for old music to reissue. The new technology made it possible to take music from historic 78s or out-of-print LPs and "remaster" the material for CD. Suddenly even casual listeners had access to blues singers from the 1920s, jazz singers of the 1930s, old Broadway musicals, and early rock and roll. You didn't even have to buy the CDS; you could hear Bessie Smith and Elvis Presley in clothing stores, hair salons, and restaurants. Popular music had always been the music of "today," but now it had become the music of "yesterday" also.

Digital Synthesizer

The sound that surrounds Madonna's voice on her albums—that smooth, perfectly pulsing, multilayered accompaniment—is due to a new toy in the studio, the digital synthesizer. Synthesizers, or machines that generate and modify sound electronically, had been around since the 1960s, but instruments based on digital technology were a product of the 1980s. By operating a few buttons and pressing the keys on a pianolike keyboard, a person with limited instrumental ability could approximate the sound of virtually any instrument and even create sounds that didn't exist before.

With the addition of MIDI (musical instrument digital interface) in 1982, one could make the digital "synth" speak to another synthesizer, computer, drum machine, or sequencer (a kind of sound controller). Fewer musicians, but more engineers, were needed in the studio: Madonna used five engineers on *Ray of Light*.

small and thin, she had a good sense of rhythm. She sang songs that were right for her: simple pop songs with likable tunes and straightforward lyrics. Her concerts were spectacles, with nonstop dancing by her and others, frequent and bizarre costume changes, and songs transformed into minidramas.

Madonna was as much a visual phenomenon as an aural one. Music video was the new pop medium in the 1980s, and she exploited it brilliantly, releasing as many as six stunningly produced videos a year and changing her image completely for each one. She was a Marilyn Monroe look-alike in *Material Girl*, then a working girl in a punk haircut, then an eager bride, a ruler of the universe, and a striptease dancer. People joked that Madonna changed her persona—and her hair color—every month, but the jokes probably masked a certain uneasiness. "There was a sense that Madonna was doing something so new and so strange that one didn't know whether to call it beautiful or grotesque," wrote social critic Camille Paglia.

Time and again, Madonna, by keeping her eyes and ears open, put her finger on the pulse of popular culture and figured out what people wanted before they knew themselves. Her business instincts were extraordinary. At every turn she knew exactly what to do to get where she was going. While other women in pop music let their careers be run by others, usually men, Madonna was always the one in charge of her own career. When *Forbes* magazine named her the nation's top-earning female entertainer of 1990—the year she earned $39 million—it came as no surprise to anyone who had followed her career. The 1980s was a politically conservative, materialistic decade. Business was booming, and material well-being was, to many people, more important than fighting injustice or other social ills. On the other hand, crime and homelessness were on the rise, and President George Bush, elected in 1988, called for "a kinder, gentler nation." Madonna, with her vast, quickly accumulated wealth and her "in-your-face" attitude was, in many ways, a suitable representative of a greedy, opportunistic decade.

Madonna had started with nothing—or, to be exact, thirty-five dollars. That's how much money she said she had when she arrived in New York City at the age of nineteen. Trained as a dancer, she had never played an instrument or sung with a band. Five years later she had an album with a major recording company, which eventually sold a staggering 9 million copies worldwide. To Madonna, it was only a start. "I always want more. That's me," she said.

Madonna was born Madonna Louise Ciccone in Bay City, Michigan, on August 16, 1958. Her unusual first name came from her mother, also named Madonna. Growing up in Pontiac, Michigan, Madonna was the oldest daughter of six children, and seemed to be her father's favorite child. He was a strict man and devoutly Catholic; the Ciccone children went to church every morning before school. When Madonna was five, her mother died after a long battle with breast cancer. The family never discussed the death, and Madonna has struggled with the loss of her mother all her life. As a five-year-old child she coped by trying to get attention. At home she danced on the table; at school she swung upside down on the jungle-gym bars to show off her panties to the boys. "I wanted to do everything everybody told me I couldn't do," she said.

Three years later, when her father remarried one of the family's housekeepers, Madonna refused to accept the woman as her stepmother. Two more babies came along, adding to Madonna's responsibilities. "I really saw myself as the quintessential Cinderella," she said. "You know, I have this stepmother and I have all this work to do and I never go out and I don't have pretty dresses."

Into this troubled picture flew an unlikely angel, a dance teacher named Christopher Flynn. Madonna, who had been taking jazz dance lessons since she was about ten years old, enrolled in Flynn's ballet class as a teenager. She had to work very hard, but the class transformed her. "Before I started feeling devoted to dancing, I really didn't like myself very much. When I started having a dream, working toward that goal, having a sense of discipline, I started to really like myself for the first time." Flynn introduced Madonna to a larger world of art museums and discos, and became a lifelong friend. "She was always trying to be better, always positive, always filled with urgency, always making the most of it, and she had this tremendous thirst for everything," he said.

After early graduation from high school, Madonna went to the University of Michigan to study dance. Two years later, she was restless and, with

Flynn's encouragement, she dropped out of college and flew to New York City in July 1978. She arrived with thirty-five dollars and took a taxicab to Times Square. Wandering around the city in a heavy coat and carrying a suitcase, Madonna attracted the eye of a man who invited her to stay in his apartment. With no apparent thought of the possible danger she was placing herself in, she accepted his offer, and he fed her and showed her around the city for two weeks.

Time and again, Madonna sought attention, usually from a man, got what she needed, and moved on. Remarkably, she was never taken advantage of. The useful men included Dan Gilroy, a musician who taught her to play instruments; Mark Kamins, a disco disc jockey who helped get her a recording contract; and John "Jellybean" Benitez, another DJ who introduced her to the dance-music world. Many of these relationships were romantic. Was Madonna being a calculating man-user or just one street-smart lady who made the most of her connections? "All of my boyfriends have turned out to be very helpful to my career, even if that's not the only reason I stayed with them," she said.

Madonna applied for and got a scholarship to study with the Alvin Ailey Dance Company, but left after several months because she needed money. She sold doughnuts, waitressed at fast-food joints, and worked as an artist's and photographer's model, posing nude. Sometimes she had a grungy apartment to go home to, sometimes she slept on friends' sofas or in music studios after the musicians had gone home. She lived on yogurt and peanuts and pop-

Madonna looking "like a virgin": a provocative cover for a provocative album.
(© 1984 SIRE RECORDS COMPANY)

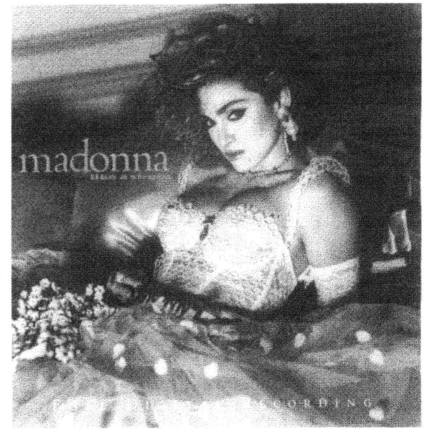

corn, supplemented by foraging in garbage cans. Or she'd get a man to invite her to dinner, and then ask to borrow one hundred dollars. "I have always been able to get my way with charm," she said.

Moving in with Dan Gilroy in 1979, Madonna began learning how to play guitar and drums. Soon she was in Gilroy's experimental rock band, called the Breakfast Club, as a vocalist and drummer. Every morning she was up at eight o'clock and, after a quick cup of coffee, she would be talking on the phone, building contacts with everyone from the local record-store owner to topflight managers. She practiced four hours a day on the drums, and two hours on guitar. She wrote songs. "It was one of the happiest times of my life. I really felt loved," she said. But when the band wouldn't let her sing as much as she wanted, she left to start her own group.

With an old boyfriend from Michigan, drummer Stephen Bray, Madonna put together a band and some demo tapes—music with a strong beat, like the Motown music she had grown up hearing on the radio in the sixties. To promote her music, she would hit the clubs, ask the DJs to play her music, then dance up a storm with her friends. She had a way of drawing attention to herself and raising the excitement level in the club at the same time. At one club, Danceteria, her song "Everybody" inspired such a dancing frenzy among the patrons that DJ Mark Kamins felt "she had an aura" and agreed to help her get a recording deal.

"Everybody" was released as a single on Sire Records in April 1982, and it was an immediate hit in the clubs. In the lyrics, in which she is irrepressibly upbeat, she wrote, "Everybody / c'mon dance with me / Everybody / get up and do your thing." Soon Madonna was dating one of the hottest DJs in town, John "Jellybean" Benitez, who DJ'd at the Funhouse, a Latino disco. He remixed certain songs on her first album, *Madonna*, adding new guitar parts and vocals and tinkering with the overall sound. "Physical Attraction," "Holiday," and "Lucky Star" owe their crisp, sparkling sonority to Benitez.

At this point Madonna had no manager—not to mention an accountant, lawyer, or bank account. She decided to go straight to the top, to see the manager of the biggest star of 1983, Michael Jackson. "I forced myself into [Freddy DeMann's] office and began auditioning there and then—in front of him," she said. "He was quite dumbfounded by my nerve." DeMann took her in and remained her manager for fifteen years.

With her first checks from Sire Records, Madonna bought a synthesizer and rented a decent apartment, in that order. Her hand-to-mouth existence was over, but it wasn't until the "Borderline" single and video were released simultaneously in March 1984 that she became a "star."

Music Television, or MTV, which started in 1981, gave developing artists like Madonna a chance to embellish a song or even give it an entirely different meaning, via music video. In "Borderline," the lyric is "You just keep on pushing my love—over the borderline." In the video, a poor girl gets a modeling job with a fancy photographer but misses her old boyfriend and her old neighborhood, across the "borderline."

Madonna exploited video further by reusing and modifying material from it to make her concerts full theatrical productions, beginning with the Virgin Tour in 1985. Tickets sold out almost instantly—at New York City's Radio City Music Hall, for example, 17,622 seats were sold in thirty-four minutes. Madonna had never performed for a live audience—apart from lip-synching to her records in a club—and critics wondered if she could really sing and dance at the same time. Could she hold an audience's attention for seventy minutes?

She could. "You made me feel / shiny and new / like a virgin," she sang in a chirpy voice, dressed in a wedding gown, and sending the audience into a frenzy. People danced in the aisles. For "Material Girl," she mimicked Marilyn Monroe's big song-and-dance number, "Diamonds Are a Girl's Best Friend," in the movie *Gentlemen Prefer Blondes*, down to the platinum blond hairdo and pink gown. The ending, though, was Madonna's. She rifled the pockets of her musicians greedily for bangles and baubles and then, in an about-face, said, "I don't need this stuff," and threw fake bills into the screaming, laughing, arm-waving crowd.

After the concert Madonna sipped champagne. "I was excited," she told *Rolling Stone* magazine. "Excited and nervous." Her new career as a concert performer had gone off without a hitch. Her three albums were selling in the millions. She met and fell in love with an actor, Sean Penn, and they married in 1985. Where could Madonna go from here?

★ In ballet class at age sixteen, unlike the other neatly dressed girls, Madonna wore ripped leotards, fastened with safety pins, and ripped tights. *"Anything to stand out from [the other dancers] and say, 'I'm not like you, OK?'"*

★ Hanging out with graffiti artists in New York City in 1981, Madonna wore sneakers with different-colored laces in each shoe, a nylon tracksuit in bright colors, a leather cap, and gloves with the fingers cut off. Graffiti artists spray-painted their tag names on walls and subway trains. Madonna chose "Boy Toy" as her tag, and she had a silver belt buckle made with the name spelled out, and she wore it at the 1984 MTV Awards, with a white lace bustier, miniskirt, and a long white veil. She donned lots of accessories: chain necklaces, strings of pearls, dangling crucifixes, and dozens of bracelets—actually black rubber O-rings used in making certain types of machines.

★ For the 1985 Virgin Tour, one of Madonna's costumes included a 1960s-style jacket painted in swirling paisley, lace stockings with the feet cut off, heeled shoes with ankle socks, a purple rag tied in her hair, rhinestone crucifix pins, a purple miniskirt, and a lacy, purple cropped shirt that revealed a black bra underneath. Madonna was responsible for setting the fashion trend known as "underwear as outerwear."

★ She was a natural brunette who dyed her hair frequently to various shades of blond. *"Being blond is definitely a different state of mind. . . . Men really respond to it. . . . I feel more grounded when I have dark hair, and I feel more ethereal when I have light hair."*

★ For her wedding in 1985, she wore a strapless white dress with a billowy skirt of tulle, and a sash of pink netting studded with dried roses, pearls, and jewels. On her head was a black bowler hat with a veil. "We wanted a Fifties feeling," said designer Marlene Stewart, who also created Madonna's stage costumes.

★ For the *Papa Don't Preach* video in 1986, Madonna went minimal: jeans, striped T-shirt, black leather jacket, hair cropped short.

★ For the Blonde Ambition tour of 1990, Madonna got heat for wearing a pointy-breasted one-piece bathing suit in a shiny metallic material. "A tough outer shell at times protects hidden vulnerability," said the designer Jean-Paul Gaultier.

★ On the MTV Video Music Awards in 1998, Madonna, in a loose, black, sacklike dress, long brown tresses, and henna tattoos covering her hands and face, did a sacred Vishnu dance. A Hindu group, the World Vaishnava Association, requested an apology for what they deemed to be a sacrilege, but they did not get one. *"If they're so pure why are they watching TV?"*

She metamorphosed. Each change in her style was more provocative than the last.

In "Papa Don't Preach" (1986) Madonna played a pregnant girl who sang, "Papa don't preach / I'm in trouble deep" and announced she was keeping her baby. People accused Madonna of encouraging teenage pregnancy. She said that was not her goal: "This song is really about a girl who is making a decision in her life." Planned Parenthood of New York sent a memo to radio and TV stations asking them "to think carefully about playing this song to young audiences."

In "Open Your Heart" (1986) the lyrics are those of a simple love song—"Open your heart to me baby / I hold the lock and you hold the key." But the video gave the words a whole different meaning. Madonna played a striptease artist in a peep show, mocking the men who were watching her. At the end, she put on a man's suit and danced playfully, innocently, with a young boy.

In "Like a Prayer" (1989) a brown-haired Madonna kissed a statue of a black saint and danced in front of burning crosses. Catholics, especially, were upset, and the Pope banned Madonna from Italy, although the song's theme—doing what's right—was actually pro-Christian. The controversy was enough to cause Pepsi to cancel a deal it had with Madonna to make TV commercials in return for sponsoring her concert tour. Madonna got to keep the $5 million advance from Pepsi, and the "Like a Prayer" single and album topped the charts in more than thirty countries. Publicity—good or bad—never seemed to hurt Madonna.

Madonna riled people, and it was not by accident. "I know that I'm not the best singer and I know I'm not the best dancer, but I'm not interested in that," she said in 1991. "I'm interested in pushing people's buttons, in being provocative, in being political."

Female sexuality, pornography, and homosexuality were much-discussed, controversial subjects in the 1980s and Madonna's favorite topics in her songs. "Shine your heavenly body tonight" are the lyrics to an early song she wrote, "Lucky Star." Madonna believed in flaunting one's sexual nature, but she also had a conscience, and wisely told everyone to practice safe sex in the age of acquired immunodeficiency syndrome (AIDS). She even gave many benefit performances on behalf of organizations that supported people with

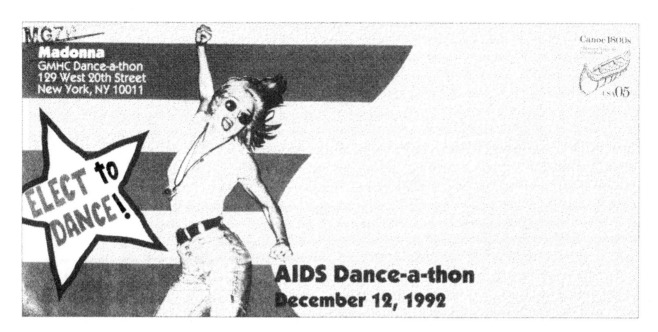

AIDS Dance-a-thon
December 12, 1992

AIDS and fought the disease, which was rampant in the late 1980s and 1990s. In other songs she explored other current issues, such as a woman's place in society, and the value of family and faith. Loss was another common theme in her songs. She returned again and again to the loss of her mother, dancing on her grave in the video *Oh, Father*, and writing songs like "Promise to Try" about how she fantasized about her mother. In an interview in *Rolling Stone*, Madonna admitted that having had her mother die when she was so young had had a profound effect on her. "She's gone, so I've turned my need on to the world and said, 'Okay, I don't have a mother to love me, I'm going to make the world love me.'" The sense of loss continued when her father was reluctant to acknowledge her success, and when her stormy three-and-a-half-year marriage to Sean Penn ended in divorce in 1989.

While music and videos continued to be her main occupation, Madonna engaged in other endeavors. She acted in movies, including *Desperately Seeking Susan* and *Dick Tracy*, and in David Mamet's serious play, *Speed the Plow*, and she acted and sang in the movie musical *Evita*. She produced an artistic, pornographic photo book, *Sex*. In 1992 she established a multimedia production company called Maverick that oversees, among other projects, her videos and sound recordings.

Madonna continued to write songs, usually in collaboration. Generally Pat Leonard or Stephen Bray composed the music, and she penned the lyrics, although she would occasionally come up with a tune and, since she hadn't ever learned to read or write music, sing it to them.

In 1991, she invited a movie crew behind the scenes of a concert tour. The resulting documentary, *Truth or Dare*, laid her bare as a fiendishly hard worker, a manipulative leader, an affectionate "mother" to her dancers, and, ultimately, a woman alone. When a friend asks, in fun, if there is anyone in the world whom she would like to meet, Madonna pauses. "I think I met everybody," she says, noticeably enjoying the joke but seeing the sadness behind it, too.

Celebrity could be a tremendous burden to entertainers in the 1980s and 1990s, when the media, responding to a perceived public hunger for information, poked aggressively into private lives of the "rich and famous." Madonna attracted the media like few others. When she got married to Sean Penn, a swarm of helicopters buzzed overhead, drowning out the ceremony. She was besieged by photographers whenever she left one of her three homes in New York, Miami, or Los Angeles.

For the most part Madonna suffered gracefully, and even, some would say, gladly. On occasion, though, the incessant ogling became too much: "I would look out my window in the [Broadway] theater and see tons of people waiting outside for me every night. And I would find myself enviously watching some anonymous woman just carrying a shopping bag, walking down the street, just slowly window shopping and taking her time, with nobody bothering her."

Underneath the brazen exterior, there was something of the "girl next door" about Madonna. She didn't drink or use drugs. She led the cast in prayer before concerts. She gave generously to AIDS-related causes. "For all her attitude and ambition, Madonna comes off pretty regular," wrote Mark Rowland in Musician magazine. "Not like she'd be your friend— she's too driven to hang out with nobodies. But if the opportunity arose, you could relate. Like Barbie, the basic Madonna model is surprisingly free of gimcracks [cheap, showy objects] and weirdness. She's fun for the whole family—a savvy woman, entering her thirties, who sings like a little girl and likes to stir things up."

In 1996, Madonna had a daughter, Lourdes Maria, with her boyfriend at the time, Carlos Leon, and underwent more changes. She practiced

MARIO TESTINO

A more introverted, mystical Madonna in 1998: "I feel that if I've been enlightened, it's my responsibility to share my enlightenment with other people."

yoga and listened to a new kind of music, called electronica. Also called "trance music," electronica was heavily synthesized, slick, and subdued, but still had a dance beat. "It was just this blank canvas, a mood thing," she said. "It occurred to me that you could take [the music] to another level by actually investing it with emotion."

Her next album, *Ray of Light*, in 1998, was another complete departure for Madonna: With lyrics that were definitely not straightforward, the album was inward-looking and confessional. In the song she wonders, "Do my tears of mourning sink beneath the sun," and says she feels "quicker than a ray of light." Gone was the chirpy voice; Madonna sang like an ordinary woman. Was this yet another transformation: Madonna the mystic? Yes and no. In interviews she talked a lot about her "spiritual journey," but in the *Ray of Light* video, she danced in a disco and showed off her belly button, just as she had done as the "material girl" of the 1980s. It was as hard as ever to figure out Madonna.

"People have always had this obsession with me, about my reinventing myself," she said at thirty-nine. "I just feel like I'm shedding layers. I'm slowly revealing who I am."

Wearing a waitress dress she found in a thrift shop, Lucinda Williams poses for the cover of the first album of her own songs, in 1980.
(FOLKWAYS RECORDING ARTIST)

LUCINDA WILLIAMS

Ramblin' Woman

A ND THE Grammy nominees for Best Female Rock Vocal Performance are: Tori Amos, "Raspberry Swirl"; Sheryl Crow, "There Goes the Neighborhood"; Ani DiFranco, "Glass House"; Alanis Morissette, "Uninvited"; and Lucinda Williams, "Can't Let Go." The TV camera zoomed in on Lucinda in her seat in Shrine Auditorium in February 1999, catching her in a half smile, looking a little nervous but defiantly unconventional in a black suit jacket and simple choker necklace. "And the winner is"—the announcer tore off the tab and unsealed the card— "Alanis Morissette!"

Ms. Morissette said her thank-yous, and the 41st annual Grammy Awards in Los Angeles rolled on with no further sight of Lucinda. Moments later, however, announcements flashed on the television screen for awards given earlier in the day. There it was: Best Contemporary Folk Album, *Car Wheels on a Gravel Road*, by Lucinda Williams.

After working in near obscurity for twenty-five years, Lucinda had won a Grammy for an album of her own songs. Taking everyone by surprise, she had beaten some better-known performers, including the doyenne of country-rock, Emmylou Harris. Making the victory especially sweet was the fact that Lucinda had labored over the album for three years, enduring criticism from the press and her fans who said she was too fussy. A *New York Daily News* critic wrote, "[The album] goes a long way toward forgiving the six years we had to wait to hear it. But then, Williams' fans had to learn patience eons ago. The 45-year-old singer has released only five albums in the last 19 years." To this and other criticism, Lucinda responded, "What's more important, getting a record out or making sure it's right?"

Lucinda likes to get things right. She's a singer-songwriter who goes to

What Is Country Music?

Most people think country music is what they hear on the country radio stations: Garth Brooks ("Friends in Low Places"), Reba McEntire ("[You Lift Me] Up to Heaven"), Alan Jackson ("Gone Country"), Wynonna ("I Saw the Light"). They're one kind of country music—"Hot Country"—or a mixture of country and pop, "careful neither to offend nor surprise," as writer Nicholas Dawidoff says.

There are hundreds of other country singers who rarely make it to radio, and never to the "country" stations. First there are the old-time country singers, the ones who started it all: the Carter family ("Keep on the Sunny Side"), Loretta Lynn ("Coal Miner's Daughter"), Kitty Wells ("It Wasn't God Who Made Honky-Tonk Angels"), Jimmie Rogers ("Blue Yodel"), Tammy Wynette ("Stand By Your Man"), and Hank Williams ("I Can't Help It"), to name a few. Only one of that group is heard on the radio, Patsy Cline ("Crazy").

Then there's the so-called alternative-country group, which includes Lucinda Williams, Iris DeMent, Steve Earle, and Emmylou Harris, who calls Hot Country "bloodless, cookie-cutter music." Alternative country is more individualistic. Its performers don't sound like pop singers; their lyrics are deeper and more wide-ranging in subject; their recordings lack that heavily produced, smooth and shiny "Nashville sound."

What all these country singers, from old-time to alternative, have in common, though, is a way of singing their words. In country music, unlike pop and rock, you can hear the words to the songs. The songs are about everyday, universal subjects—love, family, work, heartache, joy, suffering. Melodies are clean and clear, and you remember them. Country voices, too, tend to be exceptionally rich—voices you want to curl up on a sofa with.

Country music is often thought to be exclusively white, Southern, and rural ("hillbilly music"), but it is actually a stew of various styles and cultures, including urban, black, blues, and bluegrass.

The reason you can't hear Lucinda on country radio is that stations hire marketing research companies to tell them what to play, and the research is based on telephone polls using *Billboard's* country charts. Since alternative and classic country music aren't on the charts, they don't get played on the radio. In the 1990s alternative radio formats gave the music a limited hearing, but the number of stations was small: just 125 Triple A (Adult Album Alternative) stations and eighty-four Americana stations in 1999. By contrast, there were 2,630 stations playing Hot Country. At the close of the century, Hot Country was heard more often than any other music on the radio, including rock.

the depths of her experience to mine a song, and the songs are sometimes years in the making. When she produces a record, the smallest, barely noticeable accompaniment is significant to her. In concert, she keeps a black three-ring binder on the floor near her, with her lyrics encased in clear plastic sheaths, so she won't make a mistake. She hates it when the media call her a perfectionist, but she does take extraordinary care, which is why her songs and her singing stood apart from much of the popular music produced in the 1990s, when the focus was more on quick hits and megahits than on music of lasting substance. As the century came to a close, people seemed to appreciate and even relish the pause her music provided in a hectic world.

The 1998 CD *Car Wheels on a Gravel Road* sold 300,000 copies within seven months of its release—*before* the Grammy Award. Those are big sales for an artist whose music falls into no particular category and is, at any rate, far from the mainstream. Although the Grammy voters put her in the "contemporary folk" group, more often Lucinda's music is labeled "alternative country" or Americana: music that is "too country for country radio" and "too twangy for rock."

Emmylou Harris said Lucinda's voice could tear the chrome off a bumper. In the words of one critic at the *New York Daily News*, it's a "fantastically wrecked voice," marked by cracks and quavers but also by a gentle vibrato and a relaxed Southern drawl. Slim and almost waiflike, with shaggy brown hair obscuring her large eyes, Lucinda sways her hips to a slow beat regardless of the song's tempo. Her songs are spare, truthful, and often dark. The more you listen to them, the more you understand. "Just when you thought there were no more truths to be unearthed in the human heart, along comes Lucinda Williams who plows up a whole new field," praises Ms. Harris.

Lucinda Williams was born on January 26, 1953, in Lake Charles, Louisiana. It wasn't home for long. Her father, Miller Williams, a poet, moved every year or two as he pursued better college teaching positions. Soon he and his wife had two more children, Robert and Karyn. By the time Lucinda was twelve, she had lived in Vicksburg and Jackson, Mississippi; Macon and Atlanta, Georgia; and Baton Rouge, Louisiana, as well as Utah and Chile. She says she liked moving around. "We'd get to a new

Lucinda Williams, thirteen (left), with her brother, Robert, and sister, Karyn.

town and we always had rental houses, so we'd run in and decide which room was gonna be ours. I was real shy as a kid, but I enjoyed the traveling and seeing different places."

A song she wrote paints a different picture—that of a lonely, unsettled life. "Child in the backseat, about four or five years / Lookin' out the window / Little bit of dirt mixed with tears / Car wheels on a gravel road." The first time Lucinda performed that song with her father in the audience, he came up to her after the show to say he was sorry. "I didn't know what he meant, and he said, 'That song's about you. Didn't you realize that?' I was just trying to paint a picture, but he recognized me in the song. I was the child in the backseat."

Lucinda was, she said, "a pretty indoor kind of kid," living in a world of ideas, words, and music. "Even when I was five or six, as soon as I could write, I remember sitting by myself at a little table with a little chair and my little notebook, and I would write little poems and stories." The music in the family was a combination of country (her father played the records of singer Hank Williams a lot) and classical (her mother played piano). Lucinda tried to learn piano but "wasn't patient enough," she says. When a friend of her father's gave her an old, battered guitar, a match was made. She took lessons at age twelve and thirteen from a college student in Baton Rouge who taught her chords and picking techniques for folk songs like "Puff the Magic Dragon." Eventually her father bought her a better instrument, a Sears Silvertone guitar, and she proceeded on her own. "I didn't read music so I listened to records to get the melody and bought the songbooks for the chords." It was the age of folk music and the songbooks were by her idol Joan Baez and also by Peter, Paul and Mary.

One of her father's friends brought Bob Dylan's *Highway 61 Revisited* album to the house, and Lucinda was ecstatic. "[The album] brought the two worlds I knew, the folk world and the literary world, together," she said. Dylan talked-sang, he mumbled and howled. His songs were poetry: "How does it feel/ to be without a home/ like a complete unknown/ like a rolling stone." Lucinda started writing simple, introspective songs, using Dylan as her model. "I set high standards for myself early on."

Around this time her parents were divorced. She's not sure when— "it's all a blur"—but her father says she was fourteen. The children lived with their father in New Orleans. Their house was the site of frequent parties for Mr. Williams's students, fellow professors, and poet-friends, and Lucinda got the chance to play her new songs for some famous writers, including Charles Bukowski, James Dickey, and Flannery O'Connor. "They'd tell me what they liked, suggested other ways of doing things. It was like a lifetime creative writing course," she remembered. Sometimes a folk-musician friend of the family would come over and, together, with Lucinda's brother and sister, they would all sing and make music together on the banjo, guitar, autoharp, and dulcimer.

In New Orleans, Lucinda went to an inner-city high school in a time of tumult over the Vietnam War and the civil rights movement. She got suspended twice, once for distributing Students for a Democratic Society (SDS) pamphlets, and another time for refusing to recite the Pledge of Allegiance with the other students. "I'd always been surrounded by free thinkers and been encouraged to be original and stand up for what I believed in," she explained. Her grandfather was a conscientious objector in World War I and a Methodist minister. Her father was active in civil rights and supported her actions. He found an

What's New?

DVD

DVD, or the digital videodisc, which appeared in 1997, made it possible to watch movies at home with something close to movie-theater quality picture and sound. Hooked up to a TV set, a DVD player and a disc with, say, *The Wizard of Oz*, could make Judy Garland appear twice as sharp as on videotape, and "Over the Rainbow" sound almost live. The problem was, to fully appreciate DVD, you needed not only a $600 player but about $3,500 worth of other equipment (including a big TV and a six-speaker home theater sound system). Little wonder that only a million people had embraced the latest development in video by century's end.

Lucinda Williams at seventeen in her room in Mexico, with Bob Dylan's portrait on the wall.

American Civil Liberties Union (ACLU) lawyer to get her back into school both times.

Lucinda left high school for good, however, mid-sophomore year, after narrowly escaping police during a rowdy demonstration. She studied at home, and the next year the family moved to Mexico City, where authorities refused to admit Lucinda into eleventh grade because she did not have the necessary papers. In what would have been her senior year, the family moved again, to Fayetteville, Arkansas, and Lucinda was able to enroll as a freshman at the University of Arkansas. But the singing and songwriting bug had bitten her too hard to keep her there. After two semesters she left and took a job singing in a New Orleans folk bar. "I remember calling my Dad and saying, 'I know I'm supposed to come back to school in the fall, but I really want to stay and do this,'" she said. "He understood. That was the turning point. It was never, 'I've got to be a huge star.' I just wanted to be able to make a living doing this."

Making a living proved a tall order. For seventeen years Lucinda played all the twenty-five- and fifty-dollar-a-night dates she could and supported herself with day jobs. She waitressed; did filing and answered phones in offices; clerked in book and record stores; and even cooked sausages and handed them out as samples in a grocery store. She sang in some pretty unglamorous places, like the bar that put up chicken wire between her and the patrons to protect her from flying bottles. And she moved around a lot, to San Francisco; New York; Houston and Austin, Texas; Nashville, Tennessee; and Los Angeles, where she was married briefly in 1986 to a drummer, Greg Sowders.

A small, pioneering company devoted to folk music, Folkways, gave her

$250 to make an album, appropriately titled *Ramblin'*. One afternoon in Jackson, Mississippi, in 1978, she recorded fourteen traditional folk songs that she'd been singing around the country. A year later, she made another album for Folkways, this time of her own songs, with a band, called *Happy Woman Blues*.

In Los Angeles, Lucinda took voice lessons to learn how to sing correctly—specifically, to project her voice without straining it. In the process she realized her true calling was not singing but songwriting. "I was never going to be able to compete with the likes of Linda Ronstadt and all those great singers, so I thought, 'I'd better buckle down here and learn how to write songs.'"

After several hits and misses, in 1988 she got fifteen thousand dollars from an independent British company called Rough Trade to make another album of her songs, *Lucinda Williams*. The CD was applauded by critics and earned her a small but devoted group of followers. Against the advice of the British record executives, she quit her day job. "I got enough gigs to keep me going," she said. She was thirty-five years old.

For the next several years, Lucinda bounced from record company to record company as they merged, folded, or reorganized, leaving her either without a contract or with a contract, but frustrated and dissatisfied. Lucinda's saga was not uncommon in the 1990s, when a handful of major labels controlled most of the recorded music, and many, many excellent performers—veterans and newcomers alike—went unrecognized. The problem for Lucinda was perhaps more acute than some because her music, like much of the music produced in the decade, did not fit into any single category. It wasn't

Lucinda Williams playing for loose change beside her open guitar case somewhere in the Southwest in 1971.

Wynonna

"I'm twenty-seven years old and just now learning how to walk." The year was 1991, and Wynonna Judd was saying good-bye to the Judds, the duo she had been in with her mother, Naomi, for eight years, the most successful duo in country-music history. Wynonna sang lead and played guitar, and Naomi sang harmony, but Naomi was the driving force behind the duo. She made all the business decisions as well as all personal decisions for Wynonna. Then Naomi fell ill and left the duo, and Wynonna went off on her own as a solo artist.

A year later Wynonna had a first solo album, *Wynonna*, which sold an astounding 3 million copies. She struggled with the next two albums as she was plagued by fear of independence and indecision over what to sing. Making a 1992 TV special before an audience of fans, she was so frightened, she muffed songs, whined like a child, and called out, "Where's my mama?" (Reassuringly, Naomi

Wynonna Judd. (RANDEE ST. NICHOLAS)

waved from the second row.) Wynonna sought help from a therapist, had a baby, married the father, and had another baby. At the end of the 1990s, Wynonna was still "learning how to walk."

Wynonna has a large but nimble, embracing voice. It can soar to a chilling falsetto when she sings about a man "who threw her away" in the song "That Was Yesterday." Or it can be gritty and growling, as in "Girls with Guitars," a song about a guitar player who went dutifully to college, got her degree, and then defied her parents and ran away to New York City with her guitar. The song's message is: You can't stop a girl who's crazy about her guitar.

"Girls with Guitars" could be Wynonna's own story. She was born Christina Ciminella on May 30, 1964, in Ashland, Kentucky, and spent her teen years in her room playing her guitar. She lived with her mother and younger sister in a remote cabin in the Kentucky mountains without a telephone, TV, or electricity. "Music saved my life," she said. "It gave me focus, it gave me something to do, to put all my energy into."

Naomi taught her old hymns and folk tunes, and they began harmonizing: A duo was born. It took another six years of relentless hustling by the tenacious Naomi before the pair got a hearing in a recording executive's office in Nashville. For the next eight years, they were the leading female voices in country music. (Wynonna's sister, Ashley, meanwhile, became an actress on TV and in the movies.) In their songs they were assertive, sassy, resilent women. Outside the music they engaged in a searing love-hate relationship that they exposed to the public via press and television interviews.

Going solo put an end to the public display, but privately Wynonna continued to struggle for an identity as a person and as a performer. Fortunately, for all her problems, Wynonna was not a quitter. "When you get down to nothin' you got nothin' to lose," she sang in a tough, knowing voice in the song "Rock Bottom."

On New Year's Eve, 2000, she performed in Phoenix, Arizona, with her mother. The occasion marked their first concert together in eight years.

exactly country or rock or folk but had elements of all three, and record companies didn't know what to do with music that didn't wear its label like a billboard.

At one point in 1989 Lucinda made it onto a major label, RCA, but executives tinkered with the tapes she'd recorded, remixing the music to put bass and drums in the foreground and the vocal in the background. "It didn't sound like a live band at all," Lucinda said, and she walked away from the deal.

A small label, the now-defunct Cameleon, released *Sweet Old World* in 1992, and again, reviews were laudatory. The new album "cuts a deeper groove in the heart" than her previous albums, said a writer in *Stereo Review*. Her vulnerability, the writer continued, is what "separates her work from the melodrama and overblown formulas that dominate country radio."

Six years passed, however, without another record, leaving Lucinda feeling debilitated. "Creatively, I just shut down. I didn't write the whole time, which added to the stress. So not only am I broke, I can't go out and work, and I'm not writing." Giving up, though, was out of the question. "Once you've already been married and divorced and been through a couple of things and decided you're not gonna settle down and have kids, you just keep workin' on it."

Lucinda got a lucky break when one of her songs, "Passionate Kisses," was recorded by Mary Chapin Carpenter, became a hit, and won a Grammy Award for Best Country Song in 1994. Lucinda stayed home during the awards ceremony—she felt too intimidated by the idea of "people in designer clothes" judging her—but the Grammy made it easier to pay the bills, thanks to royalties earned from radio airplay (money is paid to the writer every time a song is played) and the higher fees she could now charge for performing.

Carpenter interpreted the song very differently from Lucinda. Carpenter's version is on an even, upbeat keel, while Lucinda's is layered with conflicting feelings. She starts out vulnerable, becomes demanding, and ends up hopeful and certain at the same time, singing, "Shouldn't I have all of this and / Passionate kisses." Where was the major record company that could handle a singer-songwriter with a lot to say and an edgy, uncompromising way of saying it?

Nashville, Tennessee, is called the home of country music.
(NASHVILLE CONVENTION AND VISITORS BUREAU. COPYRIGHT ◇ DAVID WRIGHT)

In New York City, Mercury Records, a major company whose roster included the 1990s teen sensation Hanson, took Lucinda on. Her next album was to have been with American, an independent label with good distribution, but suddenly American was in upheaval. With the future of her record in jeopardy, she made a deal with Mercury, which paid five hundred thousand dollars for the rights to produce *Car Wheels on a Gravel Road*.

Lucinda worked for two years on the album, recording and rerecording the songs in Austin and Nashville and then fine-tuning them in Los Angeles. "I was never really happy with my other albums, and I needed to get this one right," she said. One day in Los Angeles she reworked the song "Lake Charles," about an old boyfriend, a self-destructive type with a heart of gold. As Lucinda listened with furrowed brow, the guitarist, Charlie Sexton, tried scratchy chords on electric guitar, then twangy slide guitar, and finally, at her suggestion, slide on a Dobro, a stringed instrument with a watery sound. "Hey, Roy, how about putting some accordion on this, too!" she suggested to her producer, Roy Bittan. He and Sexton plunged into a spontaneous duet, and Lucinda cried, "This is it! This is what we've needed all along. Kind of country, but in that old-timey bluesy way. Sweet and cool at the same time!"

Rolling Stone magazine called *Car Wheels* "more perfect than the two albums that preceded it" and gave it four and a half stars, midway between "excellent" and "classic." With Mercury willing to spend money to promote the album, Lucinda could spend much of the following year on the road, performing in cities large and small and loving it. "Somewhere about two songs into a show, it starts to feel right, and I'm really happy. That's why I do this, what I live for."

She's a cool performer, a little detached, possibly a bit fearful, but also giving. In a sold-out concert in a 1,300-seat theater in Englewood, New Jersey, in 1999, Lucinda and her five-man band performed a two-hour-and-fifteen-minute set, and the audience listened in the kind of rapt silence usually reserved for symphony orchestra concerts. With a pronounced Southern drawl and a sandy tone to her voice, she sang "Drunken Angel," about a songwriter who was killed in a street fight. She delivered a gorgeous ballad, "Jackson," in which a woman travels through the South trying to forget someone: "all the way to Jackson I don't think I'll

WHAT LUCINDA WORE

★ For the cover of *Happy Woman Blues* (1980), Lucinda wore a white waitress dress that she found in a thrift shop, and held a white cowboy hat.

★ For the record jacket of her next album, *Lucinda Williams,* in 1988, she dressed in jeans, white T-shirt, black leather jacket, and heels.

★ For a photo shoot for *Rolling Stone* magazine in 1998, Lucinda wore a short red slip-dress and black boots while eating watermelon.

★ In concert in 1999 Lucinda wore black boots, black stretch velour bell-bottomed pants, a black leather jacket over a floral tight-fitting blouse, and three necklaces. Her brown cowboy hat, a birthday present from Mercury Records, was on the head of her guitarist. *"I sometimes wear a cowboy hat,"* she told the audience. *"Bob Dylan wore a cowboy hat."*

In 1996 LeAnn Rimes's first album for a major label, *Blue*, came out and immediately entered *Billboard*'s Top Country chart as number one. The CD stayed there for twenty weeks. LeAnn's debut in country music was nothing short of astounding, especially when you consider her age: thirteen.

Born in Jackson, Mississippi, on August 28, 1982, LeAnn could sing "Jesus Loves Me" at just eighteen months. At two years old she was taking tap lessons, and by the age of six she was competing in talent shows. Her parents moved to Dallas, Texas, so that LeAnn could have more opportunities to perform.

One day when LeAnn was eleven she sang "The Star-Spangled Banner" at a Dallas Cowboys football game; a local DJ named Bill Mack heard her. He gave her a song, "Blue," which

LeAnn Rimes. (MCG CURB/ANDREW ECCLES, PHOTOGRAPHER)

he had written for Patsy Cline, who died before she could sing it. LeAnn's father thought the song was too old for her ("Blue, oh so lonesome for you . . ."), but she persuaded him that she could sing the song effectively, and soon after, recorded it. A copy found its way to a Nashville record producer, and a rerecorded "Blue" became LeAnn's first hit single, and the title of her first album. She quickly set out performing on the Hot Country circuit, serving as the opening act for her idol, Wynonna Judd. "That girl is awesome!" Wynonna said. "You don't hear voices like that anymore, voices that catch your ear in a few seconds."

On "Blue" LeAnn sounds eerily like Patsy Cline, with her trademark, touching crack on key words, but in other songs she has a gutsy voice with a Wynonna-like growl. In eighth grade LeAnn sounded and looked like an adult, in makeup and figure-hugging dresses, and she sang material with adult themes, like sexual satisfaction.

"I think the reason that I don't act or sound thirteen is that I've grown up in an adult world my whole life," she said. "Those are who my friends are." LeAnn had had little chance to make friends her age, because she had been busy performing since she was six. Her touring schedule made going to school impossible after sixth grade, and she continued her schooling at home with a private tutor. More often than not, "home" was a tour bus, and "friends" were adults in the music business:

miss you much." She included a selection of gritty blues by rural bluesmen Howlin' Wolf and Lil' Son Jackson, and a tender song about her brother ("I see you now at the piano, your back a slow curve / Playing Ray Charles and Fats Domino, while I sang all the words / Little angel, little brother"). In a hard voice, she related in "Changed the Locks" how she changed the locks on the doors, changed her phone number, and changed the kind of car she drove, all to avoid a man. The song has no refrain, so its tension builds without release to the chilling line, "I changed the name of this town so you can't follow me down."

Unrequited love. Travel. Heartache. The South. Love and more heartache. Lucinda returned again and again to these subjects. She wrote on the tour bus, in a hotel room, or at her home in Nashville, anywhere she could get some time alone with her guitar. "Sometimes you're lucky and a song just tumbles out, like spitting. Other times you have to work on it," she says. To begin, she opens a purple plastic folder filled with scraps of paper containing bits and pieces of lyrics. "I sit down and see what strikes a nerve." In a phone interview with the author she described the process: "I have to go into myself. . . . I think of a hook, usually a line with a melody, sometimes just a line. 'Car wheels on a gravel road'—I had that line for a long time and let it just sit." When she finishes a few songs she makes a tape of them to send to her

LeAnn Rimes (continued)

managers, band members, other performers.

Her father, who was also her manager, pushed her to continue riding the crest of success, while her mother, concerned that she would have difficulties managing stardom at such a young age, urged her to slow down. LeAnn had no intention of slowing down, however. When her parents divorced in 1997, LeAnn stayed on the road with her father. That year, when LeAnn was fifteen, she made a reported $96 million in record sales alone. She bought a four-bedroom house for her mother and herself outside Los Angeles, with a swimming pool and a waterfall.

A second album, released in 1997, was actually songs LeAnn had recorded when she was only eleven. Called *Unchained Melody—The Early Years*, it, too, made its debut at number one, on both country *and* pop charts. More albums followed, accompanied by the highest honors a country singer could imagine: two Grammys, *Billboard*'s Country Artist of the Year *and* Entertainer of the Year.

LeAnn plunged ahead, modeling her career, she said, after singer Reba McEntire, a big name in pop-country who had taken charge of her affairs and sustained her vocation for twenty years. Said LeAnn: "My biggest goal is to stay around for a long time."

Lucinda Williams in 1999: Even "alternative country" singers wear cowboy hats, sometimes.

father the poet for review. "He's my mentor. He taught me to recognize what was and wasn't useful in a song and how revising a single word can change everything." At her father's suggestion, for example, she substituted "the hole" for "a hole" in the line "Blood spilled out from the hole in your heart." "And just that one word made all the difference in the world," she says.

With few words, Lucinda can create a picture and a mood: Sitting in a kitchen filled with the smells of coffee, eggs, and bacon, a child listens to old-time country singer Loretta Lynn on the radio. The scene changes: The child is riding in a car and sees "telephone poles," "engine parts," and "cotton fields stretching for miles and miles." The song is about being on the move. The tune is mournful, but the tempo is lazy, and her voice is matter-of-fact. Somehow the combination of all these qualities makes "Car Wheels on a Gravel Road" stab harder.

Lucinda herself has been settled, more or less, in Nashville since 1993.

She bought a house there but, uncomfortable in such permanent digs, rented it out, then lived in it briefly and, soon after, sold it. She lives in a rented house with her boyfriend, Richard "Hombre" Price, who plays bass guitar in her band. A purple Post-it sticker on the refrigerator door reads: I WILL NOT BE / MANIPULATED / PATRONIZED / CONTROLLED / TAKEN FOR GRANTED / UNDERESTIMATED. Her pal Emmylou Harris lives two doors away. Nashville is full of first-rate musicians, some of whom Lucinda picked for her band, and clubs where she can try out her songs in the company of like-minded others. But she tells just about everyone she meets that she wants to move to the desert and rent "some cheap little place in New Mexico." For Lucinda Williams, it seems, the sound of car wheels is a steady, quiet hum in her head. "I've always got one foot out the door," she says.

The following selection of compact discs may serve as an introduction to the singers. Recording company label follows title.

SOPHIE TUCKER

Sophie Tucker — Some of These Days. Flapper (Pavilion Records, England).

MA RAINEY

Ma Rainey. Milestone.
   Includes "See See Rider Blues" and "Prove It on Me Blues."
Ma Rainey's Black Bottom. Yazoo Records.

BESSIE SMITH

The Bessie Smith Collection. Columbia.
   Includes "'Tain't Nobody's Bizness If I Do."
Bessie Smith: The Complete Recordings. Volumes 1–4: Columbia/Legacy.
   Volume 5: Sony/Legacy.
   For the serious listener. The first four volumes (all double CDs) contain 154 of the 160 songs she recorded between 1923 and 1933. Volume 5, also a double CD, includes the last six songs, five rare alternative takes,

and seventy-two minutes of interviews with her niece Ruby Smith. Because of the content of the interviews, this CD carries a "Parental Advisory—Explicit Lyrics" label.

ETHEL MERMAN

Annie Get Your Gun. MCA.
 Original Broadway cast recording from 1955.
The Ethel Merman Collection: There's No Business Like Show Business. Razor & Tie Music.
 Diverse collection of songs from musicals and films.
Gypsy—Original Broadway Cast. Columbia.
 From 1959.

JUDY GARLAND

Judy at Carnegie Hall. Capitol.
 The best of later Garland, recorded live in 1961 (two discs).
Judy Garland—The Best of the Decca Years. Volume 1. Decca.
 Early material, including the original "Over the Rainbow." There's also a Volume 2.

ANITA O'DAY

The Complete Anita O'Day Verve/Clef Sessions. Mosaic Records.
 A boxed set of nine CDs. Available by mail and phone order only, from Mosaic Records in Stamford, Connecticut, phone (203) 327-7111.
Anita Sings the Most. Verve.
 A straight reissue of the 1957 LP, with the Oscar Peterson Quartet (including John Poole on drums).
Let Me Off Uptown: Anita O'Day with Gene Krupa. Columbia Legacy.
Pick Yourself Up. Verve.
 Reissue of the 1956 album, with nine extra cuts. Includes "Sweet Georgia Brown."

JOAN BAEZ

Diamonds & Rust. A&M.

Includes her best song ("Diamonds & Rust") about Bob Dylan, and other contemporary folk-rock songs, from 1975.

Joan Baez—The First Ten Years. Vanguard.

Traditional and contemporary folk songs from 1960 to 1970.

Joan Baez in Concert. Volume 1. Vanguard.

Live album from 1962.

Joan Baez—Rare, Live and Classic. Vanguard.

Boxed set of three discs, with notes by Joan, for the serious listener.

BETTE MIDLER

Bathhouse Betty. Warner Bros.

Later Bette, from 1998.

Bette Midler—Live at Last. Atlantic.

The real thing: a 1977 concert, complete with comic material.

Divine Collection. Atlantic.

Includes early material, as well as her hit songs "Wind Beneath My Wings" and "From a Distance."

The Divine Miss M. Atlantic.

Her debut album, from 1972. Includes "Friends."

MADONNA

Madonna: The Immaculate Collection. Sire.

From "Holiday" to "Vogue": Seventeen hits from the 1980s on one CD.

Like a Prayer. Sire.

Madonna's most serious and consistent album, from 1989.

Madonna. Sire.

Debut album, from 1983.

Something to Remember. Maverick.

A second compilation, all ballads, with just two tracks overlapping *Madonna: The Immaculate Collection.*

ON VIDEO:

Madonna: The Immaculate Collection. Warner Reprise.
Madonna Live: The Virgin Tour. Warner Music Video.

LUCINDA WILLIAMS

Car Wheels on a Gravel Road. Mercury.
  The CD that was on many critics' Top Ten and Top Twenty lists for 1998.
  Includes "Jackson" and "Changed the Locks."
Lucinda Williams. Koch.
  Reissue of the 1988 Rough Trade album, with six bonus tracks.
Sweet Old World. Cameleon.
  Her 1992 album.

WYNONNA

Wynonna Collection. Curb/MCA.
  Includes "Girls with Guitars."

LEANN RIMES

Blue. Curb.
  Her 1996 debut.

BIBLIOGRAPHY

A selected list of useful, interesting, and/or purely entertaining sources for the ten great American women singers in *Shout, Sister, Shout! Ten Girl Singers Who Shaped a Century.*

GENERAL

Clarke, Donald, ed. *The Penguin Encyclopedia of Popular Music.* New York: Penguin Books, 1990.

Gordon, Lois, and Alan Gordon. *The Columbia Chronicles of American Life, 1910–1992.* New York: Columbia University Press, 1995.

Millard, Andre. *America on Record: A History of Recorded Sound.* Cambridge: Cambridge University Press, 1995.

SOPHIE TUCKER

Bowers, Q. David. *Nickelodeon Theaters and Their Music.* Vestal, NY: Vestal Press, 1986.

Freedland, Michael. *Sophie: The Sophie Tucker Story.* London: Woburn Press, 1978.

Laurie, Joe. *Vaudeville: From the Honky-tonks to the Palace.* New York: Henry Holt, 1953.

Tucker, Sophie. *Some of These Days: The Autobiography of Sophie Tucker.* N.p., 1945.

MA RAINEY

Lieb, Sandra R. *Mother of the Blues: A Study of Ma Rainey.* Cambridge: University of Massachusetts Press, 1981.

Murray, Albert. *Stomping the Blues.* New York: DaCapo Press, 1976.

Stewart-Baxter, Derrick. *Ma Rainey and the Classic Blues Singers*. New York: Stein and Day, 1970.

BESSIE SMITH

Albertson, Chris. *Bessie*. New York: Stein and Day, 1972.

Brooks, Edward. *The Bessie Smith Companion*. New York: DaCapo Press, 1982.

Foreman, Ronald Clifford, Jr. "Jazz and Race Records, 1920–32; Their Origins and Their Significance for the Record Industry and Society." Ph.D. dissertation, University of Illinois, Urbana, 1968.

Gelatt, Roland. *The Fabulous Phonograph 1877–1977*. New York: Macmillan, 1977.

Shapiro, Nat, and Nat Hentoff. *Hear Me Talkin' to Ya*. New York: Rinehart, 1955.

Toll, Robert C. *Blacking Up: The Minstrel Show in Nineteenth-Century America*. New York: Oxford University Press, 1974.

ETHEL MERMAN

Ellis, Edward Robb. *A Nation in Torment: The Great American Depression, 1929–1939*. New York: Kodansha, 1995.

Green, Stanley. *Broadway Musicals Show By Show*. 3rd ed. Milwaukee: Hal Leonard Publishing Corp., 1990.

Kimball, Robert. *Cole*. New York: Dell Publishing, 1971.

Merman, Ethel, with George Ells. *Merman*. New York: Simon and Schuster, 1978.

Merman, Ethel, as told to Pete Martin. *Who Could Ask for Anything More*. New York: Doubleday, 1955.

Mordden, Ethan. *Better Foot Forward: The History of American Musical Theatre*. New York: Grossman Publishers, 1976.

Thomas, Bob. *I Got Rhythm! The Ethel Merman Story*. New York: G. P. Putnam's Sons, 1985.

JUDY GARLAND

Fricke, John. *Judy Garland: World's Greatest Entertainer*. New York: Henry Holt, 1992.

Morella, Joe, and Edward Z. Epstein. *Judy: The Complete Films and Career of Judy Garland*. New York: Carol Publishing Group, 1990.

Ritchie, Michael. *Please Stand By: A Prehistory of Television*. Woodstock and New York, NY: The Overlook Press, 1994.

Shipman, David. *Judy Garland: The Secret Life of an American Legend*. New York: Hyperion, 1992.

Tormé, Mel. *The Other Side of the Rainbow: Behind the Scenes on the Judy Garland Television Series*. New York: Oxford University Press, 1991.

ANITA O'DAY

Clark, Dick, with Fred Bronson. *Dick Clark's American Bandstand*. New York: Collins Publishers, 1997.

Dahl, Linda. *Stormy Weather: The Music and Lives of a Century of Jazzwomen*. London: Quartet Books, 1984.

Halberstam, David. *The Fifties*. New York: Fawcett Columbine, 1993.

O'Day, Anita. *High Times, Hard Times*. 3rd ed. New York: Limelight Editions, 1989.

Simon, George. *The Big Bands*. 4th ed. New York: Schirmer Books, 1981.

JOAN BAEZ

Baez, Joan. *And a Voice to Sing With*. New York: Summit Books, 1987.

Baez, Joan. *Daybreak*. New York: Dial Press, 1968.

"Sibyl with Guitar." *Time*, November 23, 1962, 54–60.

BETTE MIDLER

Baker, Robb. *Bette Midler*. New York: Popular Library, 1975.

Michener, Charles. "Bette Midler." *Newsweek*, December 17, 1973, 62–67.

Spada, James. *The Divine Bette Midler*. New York: Macmillan, 1984.

Waldman, Allison J. *The Bette Midler Scrapbook*. Secaucus, NJ: Carol Publishing Group, 1997.

MADONNA

Bego, Mark. *Madonna: Blonde Ambition*. New York: Crown Publishers, 1992.

Rolling Stone, eds. of. *Madonna, the Rolling Stone Files*. New York: Hyperion, 1997.

Sexton, Adam, ed. *Desperately Seeking Madonna*. New York: Dell Publishing, 1993.

Skow, John. "Madonna Rocks the Land." *Time*, May 27, 1985, 74–76.

LUCINDA WILLIAMS

Bufwak, Mary A., and Robert K. Oermann. *Finding Her Voice: The Illustrated History of Women in Country Music*. New York: Henry Holt, 1993.

Friskics-Warren, Bill. "Setting the Record Straight." *no depression*, July–August 1998, 56–67.

Mundy, Chris. "Lucinda Williams' Home-Grown Masterpiece." *Rolling Stone*, August 6, 1998, 39–44.

INDEX